SO-AXJ-417

The GUY'd Book

**Why we leave the seat up
... and other stuff**

To Peggy
Keep writing
and reading;
ectors is
cool, too

Norm Cowie

www.normcowie.com

Norm Cowie

Humor Writers of
America™

All rights Reserved.
Copyright © by Norm Cowie

Contact Norm at n.cowie@comcast.net
www.normcowie.com

All rights reserved. No part of this book may be used or reproduced in any
manner whatsoever without written permission, except in the case of brief quotations
embodied in critical articles and reviews. For information address Norm Cowie at
n.cowie@comcast.net

PRINTED IN THE UNITED STATES OF AMERICA
ISBN 1453664203

What they say about Norm's books

"I loved this book, fangs and all." ~Best selling author James Rollins, on Fang Face

"... an amusing teen vampire tale..." ~~Five starred review, Harriet Klausner, Amazon's #1 book reviewer on Fang Face

"... humorous fantasy at its best..." ~~ Armchair Interviews (Amazon Top reviewer), on The Adventures of Guy

"No topic is safe from Cowie's incredible wit and entertaining turn-of-phrase." Pop Syndicate (The Adventures of Guy named one of Pop Syndicate's Top Ten Books of 2007)

The Next Adventures of Guy voted
Winner of Preditors and Editors Readers Choice Award for best Sci-Fi Fantasy

"...hilarious mishaps...." Joliet Herald News

"Hilarious, witty and oozing with snappy sarcasm..." 3Rs Bits, Bites & Books on The Adventures of Guy

"Don't bother picking up this one if you've no sense of humor" Amanda Richards, Amazon Top Reviewer, on Adventures of guy

"Everything in the book is so true, you can't help but laugh in agreement." Roundtable Reviews

"...LOL funny" Beverly at Publisher's Weekly

"... profound, funny and persistently entertaining read from first page to last." Midwest Book Review on The Adventures of Guy

"... fantastically funny." BookLoons on Fang Face
"This book sucks ... in a most delightful way. Don't miss this gem..." Shane Gericke, national bestselling author, on Fang Face

3

DEDICATION

This book is dedicated to women. Kudos to you for putting up
with us.

(If you're a guy, you can use anything you'd like in here to defend
yourself if you are accused of being a guy.)

The Guy'd Book
Why we leave the Seat Up
... and other stuff

Fourword, er, Foreward, um, Foreword

The Oprah Book Club is an excellent source where you can learn about wonderful, sensitive and emotional new books that will warm and feed your soul .... that is, uh, if you're a woman.

Just don't expect to see a guy with a Chicago Bears sweatshirt in that section of the book store. Because if you do, it's only because his wife sent him there to pick up a book. Then he'll scurry up to the counter with the book folded up inside a Sports Illustrated magazine.

He's a courageous soul, though. He buys the book even though he knows that his wife will read it, and who will wonder angrily why the guy drooling in bed next to her can't be as wonderful as the guy who writes love letters and mails them in sealed bottles to a deceased wife whose post office box is in the Atlantic Ocean.

Why is this? How come a guy isn't affected by the same kind of stuff that makes a woman feel comfort, companionable, dare I say emotionally nourished? What does he get out of box scores and slow motion replays that he can't get from a good Nicholas Sparks book or American Idol season?

The Guy'd Book to Guys offers the yang to the yin, a squinty-eyed look at the universe from the perspective of one who love tools, sports and stinking up the bathroom. Learn how we guys are more sensitive than given credit for (and why we hide it), and how we adroitly mix mandatory ESPN viewing with fathering aliens, er teenagers, and partnering with one who is never wrong.

Why am I the right guy to write this? Well, any guy could, since most guys wonder about life, the universe and how to stir our latte. Then they move on, because all of this wondering makes their heads hurt. Well, I'm not afraid of hurting my head.

So come on in, and see what guys think about. See why guys only feel safe while surrounded by tools or barricaded in the bathroom (if he can ever get a turn) accompanied by the Sporting News and man-stink. See why guys spend more time in the doghouse than their dogs. Why a married guy'll put the bathroom seat down, even if he's alone in a men's room. It's about family, sports, baldness, testosterone, God, sex, fears, misconceptions, preconceptions, conceptions, and everything else that I could think of.

It's incomplete, though, since, after all, I'm a guy.

(if you read Cynic Magazine, you may have seen some of these before, including in their 'Best of' editions)

Chapter 1 Guy traits

There are a lot of different things that go into the chemical makeup of a guy, besides a couple brewskies. Here are a few.

Guts

I looked down. The ground was about a mile away. My best friend Bernie was perched on the branch next to me. We were both twelve years old and bright-eyed and bushy-tailed, or bright-tailed and bushy-eyed.

"Betcha you don't have the guts," he said, and his fingers tightened fearfully on the trunk.

So much for being my best friend.

Still, though, he was right, I didn't have the guts. I did have the stupidity, though, so I retorted, "Oh, yeah?" And jumped.

The nice thing about being young and stupid is that you are young and stupid. Young enough to heal quickly. And stupid enough not to realize that a twenty-foot jump out of an oak tree into a three foot pile of hastily assembled leaves could maim you for life, or worse, fill your tidy-whities with grubs, spiders and other nasty beasties who make their homes in leaf piles.

As a guy gets older, he loses the bravery that comes from cluelessness, so he begins to search out other sources of bravado. Or better, ways to reclaim the cluelessness that generally disappears with age and experience.

That's where beer comes in. It gives you guts. And a gut.

Because if you accumulate enough beer, you accumulate something else called a belly. This belly demonstrates to the world that you possess the guts to do mind-numbingly stupid things like jumping off bridges, bungie jumping, seeing how many cookies you can stuff in your mouth at once, or telling your wife that her new pants make her butt look big.

It also helps turn your body from a lean, mean athletic machine to a round, mound bouncing wound, a cushioned shape far more suited to protecting vital innards from the results of "ISA," or Incredible Stupid Acts.

I think that's where the phrase "intestinal fortitude" comes from. After all, bravery doesn't come from the act of eating, which is what the intestines are primarily in charge of. Rather, it comes from the beer that travels through six miles of intestines, never stopping for directions, because no self-respecting guy or beer would, then leaping bravely into the blood stream, to travel up to the brain and smother the frontal lobes with an anesthetic alcoholic phog that renders them incapable of protesting or preventing gallant acts of stupidity.

If you see a guy waddling around proudly with a tee-shirt that boasts "I'm with stupid" (with an arrow pointing up at his own face) stretched tightly over a huge taut belly, you know that you're looking at a guy who's willing to do anything on a dare, a whim or sheer capriciousness. Especially once prompted with enough ale to numb the senses and diminish brain activity, particularly in that part of the brain concerned with keeping the body alert and healthy.

So if you see a guy like this, hand him a beer and point at a nearby lake, tree, pool balcony, or hill, and say, "Betcha you don't have the guts..."

Liars

As we all know, telling the truth comes easy to guys.

In fact, we deserve praise and adulation for our absolute refusal to tell falsehoods, even when the truth is so much harder to believe. But it's all we have that really counts. Our integrity, you know. Like it's really true that I was bitten on the nose by the rare winter mosquito. No way is it a zit.

And, contrary to rumor, I never get gas. Is it my fault that the dog gets all bloaty after I eat a couple tortillas with extra-hot spicy sauce? And when the dog's not around, there's some kind of atmospheric condition that fogs everybody's glasses.

I'm a guy, I'm good at science. Why would I deny this with such a flimsy excuse? Can I help it if we keep driving though towns that smell like Gary, Indiana? And is it my fault that when the windows are hastily opened, evidence suggests (falsely!) that the smell did not, in fact, originate from outside of the car?

We don't get dogs because they help camouflage our stink. Dogs are our best friends because they are faithful and loyal. And they stick with us because they love and are bound to us, their Alpha males; not because they can tell what we ate from six feet away without having to stick their noses in our, um, opposite end.

Yeah, we guys watch beer commercials because we are seriously researching switching brands, not because of the scantily clad women in the commercials. We really do buy magazines just for the articles. Everybody knows mirrored sunglasses at the beach do a better job of repelling sand and sun. And of course, we had to go over the speed limit, because we had to get in front of the guy to warn him that his brights were on.

And forget how soap disappears faster from the women's restrooms. We guys all wash our hands afterwards. I swear. We're just more economical in our use of soap, because, as we know, soap comes from the rare and almost extinct Zest worm. We're helping nature.

I think women have a lot to learn from us. Don't you?

Why do they really have to go to the restroom in pairs? What is it about panty hose that they can wear what basically amounts to shorts in Chicago winters? And what's with Oprah? Guys don't get Oprah.

9

Finally, there're chick flicks. Nobody actually prefers a chick flick to a great special effects movie. We'd all rather watch our back hair grow, right? So what are they trying to do to us with these movies? Is it some kind of insidious mind-altering thing?

Yep, I think it's pretty clear that we guys have it over women in the old truth-telling thing. We aren't sneaky and insidious. There's no subplot here. You get what you see with guys. We are moral, with exemplary hygienic standards.

Whoa, I gotta move, the dog just let one go.

Reality Show Hell

"So, what's the problem?" he asked.

"Well," I said, shifting on the couch, "frankly, I'm in Reality Show Hell."

"And how's that?" he asked, peering down at me.

"It started pretty innocently. Sandy and the kids would be watching a show, while I'd be watching the game over in the Guy's Room."

"The Guy's Room?"

"Yeah, Guy's Room. You know, flat screen television, overstuffed chair, a bench seat from the original Comisky Park, beer, minor league baseball pennants and an Indianapolis Colt life-size replica helmet. A guy's gotta have a Guy's Room."

"Nice."

"Sure is. Anyway, during time-outs and half-time, I'd go over to see what they're watching."

"Okay, and then what?"

"You know, I'm trying to be the Modern Husband and Father, and get all involved in what they're doing and everything."

"Admirable. It's nice that this age has spawned the advent of fathers taking an interest in their families."

I squirmed a bit on the sofa, sliding a bit on the slick leather.

"Uh, yeah, I guess," I answered. One of my belt loops hooked on one of the sofa's buttons. I tried to pry it off without him noticing.

"So the problem?" he prompted.

"I dunno, I'd sit down, start watching the show with them. You know," I said, looking back at him, "I'm really not sure I can talk about this."

"It's okay, you don't have to say anything that you don't want to. Although, you will have to face your fears in order to overcome them."

I shot him a quick glance. Crazy quack. What the hell was I doing here?

"Uh, that's not it, really.." I faltered.

"Then what is it?"

I took a deep breath.

"Well, I'd get hooked on what they were watching, sometimes..." I was still hooked to the couch, and the button was coming loose.

"Yes?"

"Oh, sorry. Anyway, sometimes I'd get hooked on what they were watching, and I'd, uh, forget about the game."

"You'd forget about the game?" He sounded upset.

"Uh, yeah, I guess."

"So what kind of shows would they be watching?"

"That's what I was trying to tell you. It's all reality show stuff."

"Reality show?"

"Yeah, it started innocently enough. You know, stuff like *American Idol.*"

"Clay Aiken?"

"You know Clay Aiken?" I asked. Shocked, I twisted in the couch, and felt the couch button pop off.

"Well, uh-hem, I, uh, know the name," he said, refusing to meet my eyes. "I, uh, treat many women patients, too."

"Oh." I settled back down, parking my butt to hide where the button had popped off.

"Then what?"

"Anyway, I started watching *Survivor*. Then I got sucked into *The Osbournes*, and *My Big, Fat Obnoxious Fiancé*. It wasn't long before I was watching more reality shows than ESPN!!"

He was quiet for a few moments.

After a few more moments, I finally turned around.

He had disappeared.

There was an open door in the back, and carefully I crept up to it, and peered in.

To my shock, I saw him covertly watching, (gasp), *My Hypocritical Hippocratic Oath-taking Doctor*.

When I left, I didn't bother telling him about the busted button. For what he gets paid, he can replace it himself.

Contact Sports

Before I met my wife Sandy, I played a lot of sports; and learned early it's hard to chase down a fly ball when your glasses are jiggling on your nose. So one summer, I decided to get contacts. I made an appointment and bravely went to the optometrist's shop.

You need to understand, though, that I was a real wimp back then, when it came to needles, my eyes and road wrecks. I was squeamish about touching my eyeballs, but figured maybe there was a trick they could clue me in to.

So, marshalling my courage one bright sunny day, I sauntered into the store like I was unconcerned.

No big deal.

Just coming to pick out a pair of contacts.

Yep, just like anyone else.

Sure.

To my delight and horror, the person who waited on me was a fox!! Er, um, a very good-looking woman. I told her I wanted contacts, so she took me back to the fitting room. She took a couple of tiny bottles off a shelf, and said she'd fit them to me to see if I was a good candidate for contacts. She added that there was no prescription on these contacts, so they wouldn't do anything to clear my vision.

Then, without any warning, she shoved up on my chin, forcing my face upwards, and deftly popped a contact into each of my eyes!

She let my chin go, and I sat there, feeling disoriented from the swift movement, the bleary vision, and the feeling of the contacts sucking on my eyeballs. Next thing I knew, I was on my back on the floor, trying to struggle up to a sitting position.

She was there, and to my utter embarrassment, told me I'd fainted.

My face burning, I weakly told her that guys don't faint, we pass out.

Then I asked what had happened to the contacts. I nearly melted into the floor when she told me that while I was passed out, she had simply opened my eyes and slipped them out.

Did she do anything else to me while I was out?!

Not that I would have minded, but, like any guy, I'd rather have been awake.

Pain Threshold

When my ankle turned over, there was a little 'pop,' and I went down, imagining surgery, casts and a long recovery. My daughters, who had been watching my one-on-one basketball game against the neighbor boy in my driveway, shrieked in unison, and ran up as I rolled on my back, clutching my foot.

"I'm all right," I said, through clenched jaw. "Go get me an ice bag, okay?"

Lauren wheeled, and raced toward the house.

"And don't tell Mom!" I pleaded as she ran inside.

Because this was what was important. That Sandy not find out, if at all humanly possible. This, because the last thing she said when I strolled confidently out the door, basketball in hand, was, "Don't get hurt. You aren't a kid, anymore, you know."

And my smart-alec response flashed before me, "Yeah, yeah, right. Don't worry."

It was too late anyway. Honing in with fine tuned mom-wife radar, she was at the window, shaking her head sadly, watching Mr. Manly Strutting Guy rolling in the grass, trying not to cuss in front of his twelve-year old.

Meanwhile, the ice pack arrived, and I wrapped everything up really tight over my shoe. Bravely, I gained composure, and tested the ankle.

Waves of agony.

Nah, not really. But I'm a guy, and as such, have a guy's low pain threshold. It hurt, but I thought I could walk.

So I lurched to my feet, and hobbled to the house, trying really hard to make it look like I was walking funny just for a joke. Because it was one of those times where it wouldn't serve to be a big, fat baby, looking for sympathy. It wouldn't do any good. Sure, Sandy would doctor me, but I'd be getting the "told you so" look the whole time. She wouldn't say it, but she would think it at me, very loudly and very clearly.

Since she clearly had witnessed everything, I went into the living room and jacked my foot up on a pillow. She gave it a look. Then she gave me a look.

"So I guess you can't take the girls to play tennis," she asked archly.

Oh, yeah, I groaned to myself. But my face gave away nothing. I did a brief mental inventory of my steadily throbbing ankle. Then I twisted a smile on my face, and said, "Sure, we'll leave in fifteen minutes."

I tried to ignore her skeptical look.

Meanwhile, I wondered. How'd she know I was going to get hurt?

Was it some kind of weird clairvoyance or something? What is it about women that they always can tell in advance when something bad is going to happen?

"Get a jacket on, or you'll catch cold."

"You'd better clamp that down, or you'll smash your finger with the hammer."

"Don't get hurt. You aren't a kid anymore, you know."

I wouldn't mind so much, if they could put this ability to good that would really benefit a guy.

You know, like maybe during March Madness, maybe at the track, or when the dog's about to let one go.

Denial, a form of self-defense

One of Sandy's favorite accusations is that I'm in denial. This is mostly true, but of course I deny it. When I'm sick, usually I convince myself I'm not. I'm **placebo-incarnate**!! You could cut off my foot, but if there's a softball game going, you'll see me sprinting around the bases like a frog in a blender. Sports overcome any sickness. Just ask Cal Ripken.

Sandy hates it when I'm in denial, but curiously, it's okay if she can wrangle an admission from me agreeing with her.

"We're lost!" she exclaims.

"No we're not!" I reply hotly.

Sandy retorts, "Then how come we're passing that same hair salon again?" (women notice hair salons)

"Okay," I admit, "We're lost. Are you happy now?"

Strangely, she was. She didn't care that we were lost. She just wanted me to admit it.

Germ Warfare

Something we believe in without seeing, besides wind and God, is germs. We don't have any trouble in believing in these nasty little critters, since, without permission, they are capable of entering our bodies through various orifices, push a couple of our internal buttons, and make gobs of icky, slimy stuff ooze from and clog these same orifices, causing much mental and physical torture. Sometimes a little science knowledge is more harmful than helpful, and knowing what I know about germs is making me a twitchy, paranoid, frightened little coward.

I read somewhere that when you tinkle in the potty, the force of the pee stream is enough to cause millions of droplets to splatter upwards, like Mary Poppins without umbrella, onto and into anything above them in that particular airstream. If you're a guy, this is your hands and nose! This concerns me!

I hate to rat on Guy-dom; but if there's one thing that bothers me, it is guys who don't wash their hands after going potty! And when you shake hands with someone, you can't see if his hand is acting as a carrier for dissolved pee droplets. I look warily at the hand of someone offering his hand, always wondering if he's been giving a pee droplet a ride.

Sometimes I'm so distracted by this, I get caught by a 'hard-shaker' or a 'finger-shaker.' A hard-shaker is someone who tries to wrench your arm out of your socket. Obviously, he has some devious use for your arm, and knows if he yanks and shakes hard enough, he might just pop it off. The finger-shaker always squeezes before you reach the actual handclasp position, ending up with four of your fingers being ground together in his hand.

What has happened as a result of this, is the evolution of defensive shaking techniques, such as the 'thrust shake,' where you stab your hand forward to be sure they can't catch your fingers. Another good defensive shake technique, is the 'weak handshake,' where a macho guy is fooled into thinking he is shaking a feminine-type guy's hand; whereupon, he hastily drops the proffered hand.

The real crowd-pleasing defense is the 'clammy wet handshake,' which usually provokes a mongoose type counter-defensive yank from the aggressive hand-shaker. It's harder to inspire a good 'clammy wet handshake,' and you usually have to visualize something frightening, like a summer vacation road trip with your wife during PMS season.

Chapter 2   Types of Guys

I'm not going to get into every kind of guy, because, frankly, if you're a guy, it doesn't matter, we're all the same, ... expect for a few of us. Yeah, these guys. So I guess this chapter is about types of guys who aren't really guys.

Mechanically inclined guys

I was driving the other day when, all of a sudden, it happened.

Yep, the dreaded "check engine" light.

But the car was running okay, so I did what any normal guy would do. I stuck a post-it note over it, and did my best to ignore it.

A long time ago, even before Michael Jackson's first surgery, Man took two divergent evolutionary paths. Those of the mechanically inclined. And the rest of us.

Mechanics (subspecies Homo Goodwrenchious Sapiens) not only own tools, but know how to use them. They don't panic or go into denial mode when the engine thumps instead of ticks. Their houses are full of appliances and stuff from twenty years ago that still work, because they know how to fix them. A minor subsection of humanity, a mechanic would rather fix something than throw it away, as a prudent, normal, refuse-to-ask-directions or read instructions sort of guy will do.

There's an insidious reason for this un-Guylike behavior.

They aren't guys!

Think about it. Mechanics .... Gasp! ...read ... gasp again!... instruction manuals!

Do you hear me?!!!

Not only that, but they actually understand what they read! Without relying on pictures!

They wear special gunk-resistant clothes, and gird themselves with weird belts. They know the secrets for getting grease out from under their fingernails, and don't have to brush up on first aid before operating a power tool. They know that a catalytic converter isn't a kind of Lazy Boy, and there aren't any golf clubs in their toolboxes.

In other words, they are freaks.

I'm glad I'm not one of them.

I'm normal.

Well, um, normal, for a guy.

I'm no crank head. Nope, not me.

Back in high school, while all the mechanics were in shop tearing down transmissions, I was shooting hoops or hanging with other non-mechanics, watching cheerleader practices. When mechanics were out testing their new small-block engines, I was watching NFL football, cutting the grass, or riding my bike. In other words, while they were learning how things work, I, ... uh, ...wasn't.

The bottom line? I don't know a darned thing about how things work.

But when my 'check engine' light came on did I panic?

No way, I'm a guy. I know that quite often these things will just fix themselves. You just have to give it a chance. And if you wait long enough, the bulb will burn out, right?

I remember the first time I got a 'check engine' light. Stupid me, I did what it said. I stopped the car, popped the hood, and checked the engine. Yup, still there. My job's done, right? Anyway, a couple days later, the light went off by itself. No harm, no foul.

I like warning lights that really mean something. Oil lights, fuel warnings, seatbelt lights and the watch-it-your-kid-opened-the-damn-door warnings. These are real, and they tell you something in easy to understand pictures.

Not the 'check engine' light. Its meaning is secretive and threatening.

Some kind of bizarre mechanic thing.

Scary stuff.

Best to ignore it.

Metrosexuals

It's time to address the burning issue of whether metrosexuals are guys.

Maybe you haven't heard about metrosexuals yet. Metrosexual was a term was coined to describe those narcissistic men whose love for their own reflection is matched only by their love of a picture of themselves. Think Brad Pitt.

It's men, who not only spend almost as much time in the bathroom as my teenaged daughter, but they're doing the same thing!! And they're not in there reading the Sporting News and adding to global warming. I'm not kidding!

They're dabbing, splashing, dashing, combing, preening, and ironing their hair. Whatever that means. Their vanity is only exceeded by the amounts they spend on themselves due to their vanity.

I decided to do a little research on the subject, and go search out one of their haunts. Yep, a salon. Not a saloon. A salon.

I'm lying, Sandy had sent me there to pick up shampoo. But being a guy, I decided to multi-task, so there would be some purpose to wandering around looking for one tiny bottle in a sea of tiny bottles.

For my research, I decided to disguise myself as a metrosexual. So I trimmed my nose hair, slicked back my 'survivors' (those five hairs that stubbornly stuck around on my head, rather than migrating to my ears), then took off for Ulta, a beauty salon/retail outlet located in the foreign country of 'Mall.'

The security guard frisked me with his eyes as I entered. Not really, but he mentally cataloged what I came in with, to be compared to what I exited with. Security guard, huh? Guess you can't trust high school girls to keep from putting unpaid items in their purses. I didn't have a purse, so I must have passed mustard, er, gas, er, muster, because he let me in.

So here I was, in enemy territory. No-Mans land, for a guy. No televisions, no Miller-Lite, and, like every other female place, nowhere for hostage husbands to sit and wait while wives migrate contentedly through the aisles.

Everything was clean and bright, clearly marked and organized. Rows and rows of shampoos and soap, Earth therapeutics, bath beads, blush, foundation, moisturizer, Elizabeth Arden Overnight Success Skin Renewal Serum, spacegun-like blow dryers, hair straighteners, facial saunas, hot lotion dispensers, mascara, nail stuff, and a mini-shrine to Atkins.

After awhile, I just grabbed a bunch of shampoo bottles at random, and dumped them on the counter, asking the checkout girl, "If I glomp all of this on my head, will it get rid of my bald spot?"

She frisked me with her eyes.

No, not really, she just really looked alarmed to be waiting on a metrosexual fraud. She quickly processed my order, slipping covert glances at the security guard to make sure he was watching me carefully.

Then I escaped.

My conclusion? Uh, I don't know. What was the question?

Becoming a metrosexual

Hmm, that whale sure smells good, doesn't she?

Betcha you don't have any idea where I'm going with this, right?

It all started when I ran out of shaving cream. With the words of old commercial going through my head "Strong enough for a man, but made for a woman," I reached in the shower and grabbed the can of woman's shaving cream. As the pink stuff oozed onto my fingers, I thought to myself, if it works under tender armpits and behind knees, then it'd do the job on my chin, right? I was right, it worked perfectly. The razor glided over my skin, smoothly slicing through face hair, and there wasn't a nick, a bob, or even a tony left afterwards. And my skin was woman soft.

Awesome.

Not only that, but it left a nice pleasant scent afterwards. Some kind of subtle berry or something, that like with wine, my nose wasn't sophisticated enough to identify.

On the other hand, while I enjoyed the smell, I had to admit to having some concerns about the fragrance. Would it be safe to leave the bathroom and venture out into the world with this womanly scent hovering about Mr. Manly Me? Would my two girls catch wind, and send me running for shelter with derisive laughter, "Hey, Dad, you smell like a girl!!! Very pretty!!"

Or worse, would it add an invisible pheromone that I wouldn't know about; so when I'd leave my house, I'd be leaking an invisible trail of "Hey, Sailor!" molecules, who would be winking seductively at every male in the vicinity?

Frantically, I read through the shaving cream can, looking for the ingredient, 'whale.' Yep, you heard me, whale.

I remembered reading once that because animal musk is very similar to human testosterone, humans respond to animal musk like they would to pizza. I mean, human pheromones. And, the best place to get this animal musk? Ha! Ha! Ha! Ha! Silly you. Whales, of course. Specifically, from glandular secretions (ambergris) of the sperm whale.

Yeah, I hear you women snickering, "Oh, yeah, you men get all aroused from the scent of sperm whales, tee-hee."

Maybe. But you're the ones slathering it all over yourselves. We men are busy dabbing on musk, a secretion that comes from a pouch under the tail of a male musk deer.

Romantic, huh?

Anyway, it turned out that there weren't any whales in my shaving cream. And I was so happy with it, I decided to use it from now on. This got me to thinking that maybe I'm on the path to becoming a metrosexual.

In fact, just the other day I actually (gasp) used a pre-conditioner, then (gasp again) shampooed with my wife's expensive shampoo, before (gasp, a third time!) conditioning! Then, using a little doodad my wife gave as a torture device, er, gift, I mowed my ear and ear hair and stepped out of the bathroom looking nice, neat and trim.

And smelling like a whale.

Chapter 3 Guys' bodies

Guys come in many shapes and sizes. Most of us have bodies. We'll talk about them a little bit here.

The Burning of the Head

Late each spring, an annual event occurs to mark the arrival of summer. Around our house, we like to call it, "The Burning of the Head."

Not everybody can celebrate this event, as a certain amount of scalp has to be made available to the rays of the sun for a duration that will assure a certain doneness of cooking. This may best be ascertained when the epidermis reaches a level three (of five) on the redness scale.

Alas, those whose who sport a full head of hair, or who are chemically altered by Rogaine, will not know the pleasures of this celebration. In fact, in my case, there seems to be more and more to celebrate each year, as my bald spot morphs into more of a bald **area**.

Still, though, I'm better off than those with bald **zones**. Or those pool-cue guys, nicknamed Curly (going back to an event somewhere in the distant past), who have even (gasp!) given up the comb-over defense, after concluding that their hairless areas, like a virulent strain of weed, have taken over the garden.

Yeah. You're probably reading this, twirling your fingers in your hair, smirking at us hair-challenged people. But we are people like you. Do we not breathe like you, eat like you, burp and fart like you? We are as human as you. So stop calling us 'Chrome-dome and 'Baldy' and names like that. Because someday the secret will come out, and humanity will realize something that we already know....

(I almost hesitate to tell you)
(it's a closely guarded secret)

We ....are ....superior ....!!!

Yep, make fun of us if you want. But do you know why we are bald? Huh? Do you?

Thought not.

It's because our male hormone levels are **too high**. Yeah, take that! We are the most macho of the macho, with hormone levels jacking our manliness into the stratosphere. Boo-yah!

You think those hairy, punk, sissies, pumping all that iron, are the macho, manly, man-studs? Hah! They're worms, barely worthy of rubbing our craniums.

Yeah!

And our Forefathers knew all of this. That's why they picked the mightiest of the birds as our national bird. They even made fun of bald-challenged people by making up the Whig party, then wearing wigs to mock people with hair.

And for you deserters. Yeah, you! Do you how Rogaine really works? Forget about what you read, especially on the container. It's a lie. I did a careful study (consisting of getting on the Internet and checking out the baseball scores), and concluded that Rogaine simply reduces the level of male hormone, by **adding woman hormone!**

Nothing else makes sense, so no further studies were necessary.

I feel sorry for you guys with hair.

Ha! Ha! Ha! Ha! Ha!

Wimps.

God loves some heads, the rest He covers with hair.

Measuring Stick

I stared at the computer screen in horror, my first swallow of coffee frozen midstream down my esophagus.

From somewhere deep inside my brain, a little voice rasped weakly, "Coffee. I need coffee."

Ignoring it, my heart pounding, I punched a key to see if the little message was still there.

Yep, and now it had company. Lots of company.

Guys worry about different things than women do. We worry about the stock market, the Bear's win-loss record, how many beers we can slug before our lips lose communication with our brains.

In other words, we worry about numbers.

And what better number to worry about other than, well, uh, you know… how long our, um…

C'mon, do I have to say it???!! Are you getting the point!!!???

I never thought I had a problem. Sandy never complained, uh, back when we….but no, that's a different story.

Then it happened. The email.

Not only that, but it was quickly followed by a dozen more!!!!
Does everybody know???!!!

And they're sharing the information!!! Gathering the troops!!!! What, are they in a chat room group or something?? All talking about me???!!

So now, having researched my problem, and outing me in public, Ashlee, Kim, Carrie, Kristen, Emma, and others, are swooping down on me offering pumps, pills and patches to cure my problem. All these concerned people, acting in concert, reaching out to me with personal emails, out of all the millions of people out there. Brings a tear to my eye.

But I still wonder, how'd they find out? Did they learn of me the same way Rogaine found me out? Heck, I'm still on Rogaine's Ten Most Wanted. Or is it more sinister? Orwell stuff? Shades of 1984?

Or maybe it was my doctor. My last physical was almost four years ago. Maybe doctors forecast shrinkage based on aging and post the results on the Internet for some kind of study or something. Or maybe he's still upset I don't come back to visit him anymore after he stuck a finger in my...well, that's another story, too.

Nah, this is all wrong. I don't have this problem.

I mean, sure, I always cover up in the locker room. Don't want anyone getting jealous...ha, ha. I cover up with a washclo... no, a towe.., no, a beach towel. It takes a beach towel to cover everything.

Yeah, that's it. I'm such a macho man-stud, ya' know.

This is a mistake. I know it. They confused me with some other Norman Cowie. Yeah, there are plenty of Norman Cowie's out there, right? I, myself, know at least five others. Yeah, that's it.

Heh, heh. (whew)

Just a mistake.

Not my problem.

Now that that was settled, I got back to my email, and deleted the offers with relief.

And then I saw it.

Another email, telling me I need ... (gasp)....Viagra!!!!

How'd they know???? Have they been talking to my wife???!!!! !!!!!!!!!!

Man-stink

Guys like to stink. We all pretend to want to smell good, and we wear Old Spice and Mennen underarm deodorant, but the truth is, we like smelling bad. Think about it, women and men eat the same thing, often at the same meal; and the guy ends up with gas, which he emits without embarrassment.

I have been married for close to twenty years, and only recently found out women get gas, too. No, I didn't learn this from Sandy. My daughters slipped up when they were younger, and let the secret out, literally. I'm sure they weren't responsible, because they were too young yet for the Women-Union, which is responsible for teaching women how to train men. So, unless this is something females just do when they are young, women get gas.

I feel like a traitor to Guy-dom, but the following needs to be said: Since most women know that men don't really like to read, what real excuse is there for men disappearing with a newspaper into the bathroom for forty-two minutes? The truth is we are just reveling in our own stink. The longer we sit there, the longer the smell can permeate, until it finally starts to eat the chrome off the sink.

Also, why else do men like to go out and '...work up a sweat'? Everyone knows that the usual result of sweating is stinking. As if it's really needed, here's even more proof, look at our beverage of choice. When a guy drinks a couple brewskies, he is just stoking the gas furnace.

The only reason we even do anything at all about smelling good is fear of PMS, which science studies have proven to be set off by man-stink.

... more on this...

Some things are just so wonderfully strange that I can't do anything to embellish or make it funnier. You can just let the story stand on its own merits. And here's one that just makes me want to smirk, though I won't let Sandy see me doing it, because she'll wonder why I'm smirking, and she won't be amused by this:

On March 19, 2003 a story appeared on WebMD medical news by Jennifer Warner, and reviewed by Brunilda Nazario, MD, saying a recent study showed that the odorless pheromones found in male perspiration can boost a woman's mood, reduce her tension and make her more relaxed.

Really?!

Good news, as far as I'm concerned.

Smirk, Smirk

I gotta go.

I'm going to toss my Mennen speedstick and go sweat on my wife.

Skin

Our skins are pretty amazing. If you think about it, we are just big water balloons. Our body is more than 85% water, and everything is held in by our skin, which also keeps most things out, including telemarketers.

It comes in several colors, which is another thing that amazes me. I have more in common with a black or Asian man than I do a woman. We share many things, including fear of PMS, hatred of telemarketers, anger at traffic congestion, boredom with romance movies, and joy in a beautifully-thrown curve ball. Yet, rather than banding together, many men hate others simply because they are colored differently!

I tangent.

Another neat thing about our skin is the way it retains its shape. Try pouring a bunch of water into a balloon. See how it takes on a pear shape? Logically, this should happen to our bodies too. Yet, we are held together in a pretty bizarre shape, with almost no risk of losing this shape, other than around our waists (if we are men) and our bottoms (if we are women).

You know, we really do leak. That's what sweat is. And, contrary to thought, you should **want** to sweat! Sweating is God's way of cooling down our bodies, so when you are putting on antiperspirant you are actually preventing this. My personal studies have shown that eighty-seven percent of strokes and heart attacks are brought on within three hours of applying antiperspirant, causing bottled-up sweat to internally back up, putting additional pressure on your internal organs, fatally, or near-fatally, squeezing your veins and arteries beyond tolerance limits.

Unfortunately, the Lobby for Mennon underarm antiperspirant/deodorant has perpetuated the myth that sweating is socially unacceptable, and has stifled the truth just as the cigarette lobby did with cigarettes for so many years

I doubt we can do anything about this until the lady who poured hot coffee on herself at McDonald's decides to sue the powerful underarm antiperspirant/deodorant lobby in a class-action lawsuit.

She's my hero! She'll teach them.

Weight loss

I had another thought about leaking when I weighed myself the other morning. I actually weighed less than I did just before going to bed. Hmmmm. What's up, here? I decided to do some testing, and for the next three days, I weighed myself every evening, and then weighed myself the next morning before going to the bathroom, showering or losing more hair. Each evening I weighed between 171 and 173 pounds. But in the morning my weight fluctuated from 168 to 170.

What gives? How could I lose weight **while I'm sleeping**?

I wasn't sweating, I didn't get up to go to the bathroom, nothing happened to cause me to lose weight between the time I went to bed and the time I woke, so what happened to the extra three pounds?

Since my body is just so much water, there's only one answer, as horrifying as it is.

I evaporated!

Belly Button Lint

Does anybody else have this problem? Every day, when I peel my shirt off, there's lint in my bellybutton. I'm not overweight, so it's not like there's a huge divot there or anything. But somehow, no matter what I'm wearing that day, cotton, polyester or aluminum, I find a little colorful ball of fuzzy stuff tucked in where my umbilical cord used to be.

What gives? It's not like my bellybutton faces down, and something floats up into it, nor does it face up, so that gravity pulls something down. Since I'm vertical most of the time, my bellybutton faces straight ahead of me, on a perpendicular path to the ground. So however the lint it getting there, it has to be taking a horizontal bee-line right at my midsection.

All of these facts lead to one frightening conclusion: lint is alive! A heretofore undiscovered new life form, possibly related to the sucker-faced telemarketer since they move much the same way, crawling into a nesting place and attaching themselves.

And since lint is a life form, it stands to reason that its parents (my shirts) are alive, too!! AAAAAARRRRRGGGGG!!!!!

And think about it, my shirt has seen me naked!!!

...

SAVE THE LINT!!!!!

Only purchase dryers that come with lint free traps! Lint traps are inhumane, or in-lint-ane, causing slow death by squashing the lint against a screen, depriving it of life-giving air which is sucked out during the spin cycle. Look for dryers that display the NO LINT sign, with the little symbol of a figure that looks like Rice Chex (indicating woven fabric) with a line drawn diagonally across it.

Butts

I listen to the comedian Gallagher to get his insights into being human. He once made an observation that intrigued me.

Once, before he started bludgeoning fruit, he opined that it was wonderful that God put our kneecaps on the front. Then he wondered aloud what chairs would have looked like were our knees in back. We'd all be walking around like a bunch of big-headed ostriches.

Inspired by this, I wrote a children's book about knees. It was a very funny book, but I decided not to share it with the public, because I was having trouble with the illustrations. You try drawing a knee-character!

Anyway, this got me thinking about how silly we really look. I mean, even though I spent so much time studying women, I never really focused on the parts that make up a woman. Take the ear, for example (I didn't mean this literally, Vincent!). Look at an ear. It's a mess of folds, wax, hair (on my lifeguard students).

Sometimes it has lobes, sometimes not. It's really not very attractive. That's why we wear earrings, to distract people from the actual ear. God gave us hair to grow over, not in (though this is changing with me every year), to cover this unsightly thing. Not even the most beautiful model in the world has an ear that you could call attractive. They just aren't.

And your butt, your basic butt. For all the time men spend staring at the bottoms of women, it's not really beautiful in the way of a sunset, or a swan, or the Colts winning the Super Bowl. Yet, you will find no lack of male volunteers to drop what they are doing to gawk if the right one comes along.

31

Chapter 3 Guys and Gals

When you're dating, the whole purpose of dinner is for sex - when you're married, dinner is because you're hungry.

Gender Differences

After a lot of study about the differences between men and women, I'd like to finally offer my results. Are you ready for this? Here goes...

Women and men are different!

I know, this is so radical that you doubt the validity of my study.

Well, here's how I came to this startling conclusion. It started back in junior high school when the girls started sprouting a couple items most boys would prefer to only see on a girl. I, just a living hormone at the time, noticed this difference, and determined to study it.

With many false starts, I started making progress once I got into college. Surprisingly, some of the earliest results came from a statistics class. We were given the project of doing any kind of statistical survey we wanted, and compile our results using Z scores, bell graphs, means, modes, medians, chest size, etc. Being no dummy, I decided to do a study to determine the sexual preferences of blonde, brunette and redheaded women as to their choices of blonde, brunette or redheaded men. Notice that bald men were not included in this study, as I seemed to have most of my hair at this time.

I spent the better part of two weeks (I had to be thorough, didn't I?) canvassing women in the girls' dorms to make sure I had enough responses for a legitimate survey (the results of this study are available if you send me $5.99 plus postage and handling - yes, I like to be handled).

I continue my study of women, even now, but under the threat of dismemberment I am confined to studying just my significant other and the two test subjects I fathered. My vigilance in this study will no doubt intensify when my girls start sprouting a couple items most boys are interested in studying.

Speaking of which, I spent quite a few years in karate, and became fairly proficient, earning my black belt. I don't practice anymore, but I plan on bringing my *gi* out of mothballs once my girls start dating. Then, when I meet a prospective hormone, I mean boy, I will require that he spar with the old man before the date. After I toast his cookies, he will be sure to have my test subject, I mean daughter, back at the stipulated time.

Romance

I think I finally figured out the whole deal with 'chick flics.'

You know chick-flic's. Those sappy, emotionally gut-wrenching cry-fests that turn your wife or girlfriend's mascara into a black river that races down her cheek, leaving a track like that of a rampaging earthworm gone amuck. Meanwhile, you're staring at your fingernails, positive that you can see them actually growing. Worse, you're trying to forget that you coulda/shoulda been watching a good action film, SciFi, thriller or cartoon.

But no, SHE wanted to see the new film 'Bridges of This-Film-Sucks-County."

And you, after a minor protest (which mostly consisted of scratching yourself violently), went ahead with her program, realizing the futility of arguing with someone who, like a wolverine, is half your size but twice your ferocity.

But if you'd have known the truth, you'd have taken the risk of being bitten, because chic-flics are Propaganda! Brain washing! An insidious plot almost as evil as stealing the catcher's signs from second base. It's all part of the female master plan to introduce her Cro-Magnon to ... ah, I can't bear to say it! ..... it's just too horrid! ....
So I'll type it instead .....

Ready?

Here goes... 'Romance.'

Yeah, romance. You heard me. Now go wash your ears out, or run away screaming like a banshee on uppers.

Anyway, it's essential that if a woman desires romance, she must first lead her guy by the nose to romance, which should never be confused with sex, lust or infatuation with Monday Night Football.

So a woman does just that. She has to, because she knows we have no concept of romance. Heck, the evil consortium Fannie May Candies and Hallmark make up a calendar telling us when we should buy candy and flowers, because everybody knows we'd never get the idea on our own.

Except, of course, for those occasions where we do something stupid. And I mean something extraordinarily stupid, as opposed to ordinary-for-a-guy stupid. Like taking your daughter to the supermarket, and remembering the butter, but leaving your daughter somewhere in the frozen pizza section. Regrettable stuff like that.

That's where chic-flics come in. They are training guides for guys. Just like romance books are instructional manuals for females written in an archaic code impossible for men to decipher.

So the man and woman sit in the theatre, she enthralled by the thrashing of emotions on the screen, he sucking down caffeinated drinks in the vain hope that he might stay awake, or at least hoping that he can keep his snoring down to chainsaw level. Meanwhile, glued to Richard Gere on the screen, who dazzles the ladies with sensitivity and style, she's hoping against hope that the schmuck dribbling popcorn on himself next to her might actually pick up some kind of clue on how to really treat a lady.

You'd better forget about it. Our alleged brains don't work that way.

You want romance?

Either smear pizza all over yourself, or try to convince your guy that you are an NFL team.

Simple arithmetic

Women stink at math. We all know this, right?

Hah!

It's a lie. It's time to dispel that myth once and for all. It's all a carefully crafted fib perpetuated by the woman's lobby, R.O.M.B.R.A. (Rule Over Men By Resisting Accounting).

I learned this horrible truth by conducting an in-depth study of brownie points, the wonderful accounting mechanism husbands use to purchase Saturday golf outings, guy's nights out or long visits to the hardware store.

If you aren't familiar with brownie points, there are a few simple rules. First of all, only men can accrue them. We get them for anything we do that does not involve tools, autos or sports. Also, they must be used while they are fresh, or your wife will not give you credit.

If we pick up our own wet towel from the floor, we get a brownie point. If we pick up a towel dropped by one of the kids, two points. Coming home on time from golf nets at least two points, and if we touch a dish with the intent to clean, we get at least three brownie points. We get more if we clean windows, bonus points if it's done well enough that our wives won't have to redo them. In other words, we get credit for anything except stinking up the bathroom.

Anyway, it all started when I noticed that my wife wasn't calculating my brownie points properly. It wasn't my fault! I was doing everything to make sure I got full credit for all of my brownie points. Any time I did anything worth points, I faithfully followed the guy's rules by announcing it. "Hey, Sandy, did you notice that I cleaned up the cat barf?"

By my reckoning, this alone was worth at least one night of Wednesday Night ESPN baseball.

But when I tried cashing it in, she scowled at me and the beer in my hand. "What do you think you're doing?"

Usually, if you have surplus brownie points, they aren't allowed to do that. So I started rattling off my brownie point accomplishments. "Hey, I cleaned the cat barf, picked hair out of the bath tub drain, and changed two light bulbs this week,"

She crossed her arms, "So, I drove the kids to camp, violin and tennis lessons, registered them for school, mopped the bathroom and kitchen, did seven loads of laundry, washed the dog, consoled your daughter who was fighting with her best friend, put fifteen meals on the table and dealt with an icky call from the orthodontist."

"But you... uh, you don't ...." I sputtered.

"Then I scraped the cat barf out of the towel you used, and laundered it."

"Uh, but, um..."

"And I fixed the plumbing that you promised you'd do for the last three months."

"Uh."

I think you can see by this that she clearly broke all of the known rules by doing some sneaky, Enron-type accounting! I fully plan on bringing it up during the next collective bargaining between our unions.

Living in the Doghouse

There's a reason that a dog is a man's best friend, and it's not that we smell alike. Well, okay, maybe we do.

But it's more because oftentimes we both share the same house. And I'm not talking about the one with a kitchen and running water.

We guys get in trouble for the stupidest stuff.

Case in point. My teenaged daughter Sam was across the street at her best friend's house. It was a school night, and she knew lights-out is at 11:00. So one minute after I waited in righteous anger at the front door, ready to pounce.

Fifteen minutes later, I'm battling to keep my eyes open.

Not wanting to phone across the street, because I don't wake up any adults that might have sensibly gone to bed, I threw on a coat and tromped outside.

Then I tromped back in and grabbed an umbrella because it was raining like hell.

Then I tromped back outside, wind whipping up my shorts and rain pelting sideways like a mutant mini-hurricane.

Three minutes later we're back in my house, and I'm having a patient conversation with her, complete with bulging eyeballs, veins standing out from my neck.

She's warding me off by rolling her eyes like 'Dad, you're so stupid, and I'm just pretending to listen while I'm really humming that new song by Twobuckrapalot, and I'm not learning anything here and I'm telling you this by rolling my eyes at you."

I could yell at her for what she's thinking, but we've had circular arguments about my mind-reading ability in the past that have all ended in a draw, with her winning because it ended in a draw.

So I vented and spewed, and went to bed muttering to myself.

Here's where the stupid happened.

The next day I went swimming.

I'm usually home in an hour and a half.

But that night I got into a zone. If you've played sports, you know what I mean by a zone. Like you're out in the yard shooting hoops, and one day everything goes in. You can't miss. Fifty-foot swish. Reverse lay-up. Bomb from half-court. Everything drops. When this day happens, you don't stop. You shoot until you exhaust the zone and wear out every single swish. Dinner's ready? Forget it. Swish. Dallas Cheerleader walks by. Forget it... well, maybe a glance, then swish. But you aren't done shooting until the zone is gone.

Well, it happened to me that night. I swam like a croc, the waves parted before me like the Red Sea for Moses. I swam and swam until the zone was used up.

Four hours later, I went home.

Unfortunately Sandy heard every word I said to our teenager. And repeated every single word back to me that night.

Doghouse? Don't give me that. I'm the man of the house, you got it?

I mean, get real. Throw me a bone, okay?

Hmm, rawhide.

Smells good.

Okay, maybe just a nibble.

His-tory

"Ready to go?" I asked innocently.

Rather than responding, Sandy shot an eye dart at me, rife with menace. The hairs raised on my neck, and my bladder threatened immediate action.

"Oh, uh, take your time," I amended hastily.

With majestic bearing, she disappeared back into the bathroom.

I settled down to wait, and decided to exercise a few brain cells. Well, okay, both of them.

And that's when it hit me. Women resent guys, and here's why. We're simple.

And it bothers them that it doesn't bother us.

We express ourselves simply, "Boo Yah! Yeah! Whoa! Whoo-hoo! Wheeha!"

We like simple foods, "Just give me a steak, the bloodier, the better, heh, heh."

We don't tweeze, cram our feet into pointy shoes, wear nylon stockings in sub-zero weather, or shave our armpits. If we get razor rash, we grow a beard. If something hangs out, we let it, be it our shirtsleeves or our guts.

If we have gas, we simply release it from captivity, letting it join its gas friends in the atmosphere of our world. Then we blame the dog.

We like noise, bugs, and dirt, and we always stop to watch a fight.

Rather than 'understanding' a problem, we'll figure out a solution.

Simple rules for simple minds, huh?

Yep, that's us.

I think that's why women name everything bad that happens to them after us. Think about it, **men**opause, **hys**terectomy, **hys**teria. Others are just meant to insult, like **men**tal, **man**ipulate, **men**ace, **man**gy.

Because the secret truth is, they hate us and want to punish us for the rest of our lives.

I'm not kidding.

I mean, we should get the hint at our funeral, er, wedding day. Do guys insist that women wear white? Nope, it's all their idea. We don't care. All we care about is how many buttons and snaps we have to remove afterwards.

So what is it with the white dress? I think it's meant to confuse us, mess with our flight/fight impulse. They know we won't run away from a color that's synonymous with surrender. The white flag.

Women, pretty darned tricky creatures, pretending to surrender.

So, what is it that bothers them the most?

I thought about it while I waited at the kitchen table, listening to the little sounds of industry and progress coming from the bathroom as my wife transformed herself from, uh, the most beautiful woman in the world, to the most beautiful woman in the world.

What is it they hate about us?

Let's see. I was in and out of the shower in five minutes, and scraped the hair off my chin in three quick minutes. Dried, dressed and out of the bathroom in six hundred seconds. Nature endowed me with a hairline that facilitates quick drying, so a blow dryer is sheer overkill. My armpits, chest, legs, ears and nose sprout untamed fur. Cellulite means nothing, and I can suck in my gut any time I want to look more manly.

Ten minutes, start to finish.

They can't do this?

Oh.

...

I read once that our brain interprets things we see upside down. And it uses the same invert principle with motor skills, since the right side of our brain controls the left side of our body, and vice-versa. This invert law holds in other situations like it takes men 41 seconds to comb our hair and brush our teeth, yet it takes 41 minutes to poop. On the other hand, women can poop in 41 seconds, but it takes them 41 minutes to brush their hair.

God showed His vast sense of humor by using this same formula in sex. Men are at their horniest as teenagers, but women's fuses don't light until after forty.

Train of Thought

Sometimes Sandy wonders how we can be discussing something, and all of a sudden I blurt out something totally unrelated to what we were discussing. What happens, is my brain will take what she was saying, and go into all sorts of tangents. Tangents are in the math family, so this is normal and natural for a guy. Sandy doesn't get it, though.

For example, she asks me to run to the store and pick up some eggs. So I start reminiscing about a college physics class where two people held a sheet, making a wall with the bottom folded over into a pocket. A third person threw an egg as hard as he could into the sheet, to prove that the egg wouldn't break.

Then I naturally (at least to me) follow this thought to other interesting physics properties, like viscosity, which is an amazing property of nature where the lack of friction will allow an object (like my shoe) to sliding on an object (like ice) taking advantage of another nice law (gravity), with the result being that my back pockets smack hard into Mother Terra.

This train of thought is interrupted when I noticed that she was still looking at me, with one of **those** looks on her face.

So I scramble to remember what she had been talking about, and all I could think of was eggs. This reminded me that I have to sign up for softball (I remembered this because of the person who threw the egg).

So, I looked my lovely wife in the eyes, and I did my best to answer her question in the very best guy-way available, "Would you mind going to the Park District and signing me up for softball?"

She wasn't even proud of me for remembering that it was time to sign up.

...

I was reading once that most people only have room for seven active thoughts in their minds at a time. If a new thought is added, one of the original seven has to be forgotten, or simply placed on your mind's back burner. These seven thoughts might be as follows:

1)   We are having pizza for dinner.
2)   I get to leave work in twenty minutes.
3)   Softball season starts soon.
4)   The Orioles have no chance to win the pennant.
5)   I get to leave work in seventeen minutes.
6)   I want pepperoni on my pizza.
7)   I get to leave work in fourteen minutes.

As you can see, there's simply no room to remember that I have to pick up my daughter after work. Somehow, Sandy just doesn't get this concept. Worse, I can't find where I read this so I can prove it wasn't my fault.

This reminds me of another thing I read once. The average male can only remember three items at once for a grocery dash. If more than three are needed, a list is required. So, if Sandy asks me to get eggs (oh, no! here we go again!), ice pops and yogurt, I'm fine. But if I'm closing the door on my way out, and she says, "Oh yeah, get some pretzels," I have to come back in and make a list.

I'm sure this has something to do with the seven thoughts I discussed above. Maybe there is simply a limit to the number of items you can fit in each thought. Of course, Sandy doesn't need a list to remember lists of ten or even twenty. I personally feel this is because she clears out all seven of her thoughts, and plugs in the spaces with grocery items. She simply drops the Orioles' pennant chances right out of her mind.

Yeah, like I could do this.

Food for Thought

Sandy keeps trying to convince me that life is kinder to guys than to women. You know, the whole baby thing, time spent in the bathroom, stuff like that. So one day, she pulled out an issue of *Reader's Digest* to help illustrate her point.

It suggested five foods that studies show are good for men, and five foods good for women. Am I allowed to say 'good?' Or is it 'well?'

Anyway, men can have tomato sauce (yeah, pizza!), oysters, broccoli, peanut butter and watermelon. Not too shabby.

Women benefit by papaya, flaxseed, tofu, buffalo meat and collard greens.

While I read this, I could see Sandy looking at me, a triumphant smirk on her pretty little face.

Point, set, match, as far she was concerned.

Oh yeah, how come they get to eat buffalo?

I'm jealous.

And what's a flaxseed, by the way?

To be honest, men do really have a few advantages over women, and we'll give a few examples:
- Mens' butts don't get cold when we pee.
- Our opposite sex is women.
- Our mates don't stink.
- It's socially okay if we grow hair on our legs and backs.
- Our fat settles where it is easily covered by shirts.
- We have low thresholds of pain, so we were able to talk God into making women the child-bearers.
- If we're in the shower, and someone walks in, one hand can usually cover everything.

Other differences:
Men yell - Women scream
Men sweat - Women perspire
Men pass out - Women faint
Men fart - Women, uh, don't

<u>Fore!</u>
I just have to get this off my chest.
Golf is a guy's sport.
Whoa, ladies, stop whacking me with your purses!
Let me explain - sheesh! If you still don't like the explanation, then sure, go ahead, pelt me with frying pans.
Anyway, this thought occurred to me when I saw a picture of Mianne Bagger, a golfer at the Women's Australian Open. It occurred to me that every single one of those women would whip my butt at golf. And not only me, they would beat the Dockers off every guy I know. But you know what? That isn't the point.

Every spring when I load my clubs into my trunk, so that they are available for all golfing opportunities, whether planned or spontaneous, I look forward to everything about golf that makes it a guy's preoccupation.

I look forward to recovering from a shanked tee shot, scarfing a beer and hotdog at the tenth hole, groaning in mock sympathy when someone else's shot splashes, and real agony when mine does. I look forward to when the pretty girl in halter-top drives up in the beer cart, and suddenly everybody wants to buy the round. I look forward to that one great drive on the eighteenth that drives out of my mind the previous seventeen slices and hooks. That great drive is what brings me back the next time.

Golf is about missing par when your chip was knocked off course by goose poop, or making par because some goose poop redirected your errant putt into the cup. It's about giving your buddy advice about his slice. Or him helping you find your lost ball, the fifteenth of the day, and your last one. Then there are the handshakes after the eighteenth, where you say "Great game," even though nobody's was.

In other words, golfing is about screwing up. And I think we can all agree that screwing up is a guy's particular talent. Golf, after all, originated in Scotland, right? Land of skirts, I mean, kilts (Shut up! I can say this, my grandfather came from there on a boat). If the goal of golf was to get good, wouldn't the best golfers come from the land that created it?

When I say that golf is a guy's sport, it's got nothing to do chauvinism, which Webster defines as "...unreasoning devotion to one's sex ... with contempt for ...the opposite sex..." There's no contempt when I say that my wife would out-golf me within a year of learning to play. But she wouldn't enjoy it as much as I.

So what was the big deal about Mianne Bagger golfing the women's Australian Open? Not much, other than she's a he. Or, uh, was a he. But now he's a she, not a he. So she, not he, is now an ex-he in the 'she' tournament. Mianne is a transsexual, the first to play in a pro golf tournament. And guess what? He, uh,

she, got whipped. So did being an ex-guy give her an advantage?
Of course not. And that, my friend, is the point.

Whew, glad I got that off my breast, er, chest.

Rats

Back in college, I had a female roommate once, who took a
Psych class where they were going to be working all semester
with ... (gasp) rats!

Imagine that, if you could.

No? Okay, picture an innocent spider crawling up on the
ceiling, minding her own business, since she already bit the what
off the whom. Now imagine a blood-curdling scream vibrating
the spider so bad that it falls to the ground, catching itself at the
last instant by shooting out a silk thread line. All of a sudden, a
book bag zings through the air, hurtled by the superhuman force
of woman adrenaline and fear, with the speed of a Scud missile,
splashing the spider into abstract art on the wall.

That's Patti.

Now try to imagine the whole rat thing.

Here she thought they would, maybe at the worst, deal with
little white mice and mazes. Instead, it's rats and a chessboard.
Yep, they had to try to teach chess to rats.

You'd have to know Patti, but I could just imagine her on the
first day,

"Rats," she shrieked, "if I'd have wanted to play with rats, I'd
have taken biology."

Or dated that pre-law student.

Still, though, Patti and her classmates managed to conquer
their revulsion, and work with the albino rats all fall. Her rat was
named One-Ninety, which was the number inscribed on his metal
ear tag.

When the semester was over, and it came time to bid adieu
to their little furry buddies, Patti learned that the rates were to be

disposed of (nice euphemism for exterminated, killed, wiped out, demolished, rubbed out, squashed).

So Patti, instead of dumping One-Ninety into the vat, scooped him into her purse and brought him home.

Once there, all of her ingrained instincts returned, and suddenly One-Ninety became, not her chess partner, but a rat.

So she gave him to me. And never picked him up again,

... at least when I was looking.

You see, sometimes I wonder about this whole afraid of spiders, snakes and bugs thing. There's something about it that just doesn't ring true. I mean, just think of the Black Widow spider, who gives a pretty powerful argument for **female** superiority.

And there are other cases of female superiority. Think of the mighty lion. Who do you think does the hunting in the pride? If you think it's the one with the pretty mane, you can forget it. The lioness does all of the hunting, bringing down cape buffalo with her bare, uh, claws. Meanwhile the male lion sits around the house, eating Doritos, and making sure the cubs take their naps.

You think maybe women just pretend to be afraid, just to pump up some male sense of worth?

Hmmmmmm...

Babies

The following scenario further illustrates the proven difference between men and women: Kelly comes into work, sporting the 'Rachel' haircut (popularized by Jennifer Aniston from the TV sit-com, *Friends*), and the exclamations start, ... "Oh, Kelly! You look sooo cute!," squeals Kathy. Nancy chimes in, "You look adorable! Where'd you get it done?" Every one of the females in the office verbally adores the new hairstyle, and they cluster around Kelly like she's a baby weighing eight-pounds seven ounces and eighteen inches long (another reason for excitement in the office social sphere.)

Meanwhile, you just see guys cutting sideways eyes at the whole scene, refusing to get close enough to get sucked in for fear of being mocked by other guys. You just don't see men doing this. When 'Bob' grew a beard in the three months since 'Rick' last saw him, the most you'll hear is a low voiced grunt like, "Yeah, I grew one a couple years ago, but the wife had me shave it when the fleas got too bloodthirsty."

No way will Rick say, in a falsetto, "Bob, you look great! How long did it take to grow? Oh, and I love the way you look in that silk tie. Is it new?" The only way an exchange like this will happen is if Bob is an aggressive hand-shaker, and Rick employed the 'weak-handshake' to ward off having his arm ripped from the socket.

And about babies and baby pictures. Women converge on baby pictures like sea gulls to crumbs, or Congressmen to pages. And since every baby looks alike, why do women act like they can tell baby-Jessica's nose is just like her mother's? The closest thing like this you'll see guys doing is when a couple of guys are Oh'ing and Ah'ing over the way Alex Rodriguez is smacking the ball after bulking up over the winter.

Is there a name for that part of your back that women can reach, but men can't? You know where I mean, that tiny little area right between the shoulder blades. That spot always itches on a guy, but it's in the one place on his body that he can't reach. It's not unusual to see a guy rubbing his back on a wall, looking like a brown bear.

But a woman can reach it easily. Then they flaunt their superiority. They even put their bra hooks there! They can just whip their arms all the way around their body, and deftly hook and unhook themselves. Weaker sex, indeed! A guy would have an easier time taking off a strait-jacket than anything that hooks between the shoulder blades.

Also, you think you'd ever see a man wearing nylons in subzero weather?

Men don't cry, though some might fake it, so women think they are sensitive. When my wife and I rent movies we take turns getting Sandy-movies and Norm-movies. Sandy usually cries during Sandy-movies.

Usually, just when the hero's head is removed while he is gazing with love-swept eyes at his woman, who is in the audience staring vapidly at the executioner, who suffers from stage fright so he's imagining everybody in their underwear, Sandy whips her head around to see if she can see the merest hint of a tear in my eyes. I, seeing that this moment was coming, started concentrating on my toenails. I try to actually sense them growing, so that I would be so distracted when the tearful moment started, that my eyes would be as dry as underarms after a good dose of Rightguard.

She hasn't caught me yet, and I've become quite aware of what my toenails are doing.

Chapter 5 PMS (Pre-Murder Syndrome)

Guys are generally fearless. We usually won't admit to fear ...with one exception.

Pre-Murder Syndrome

A strange thing happened to me, back when I was still in high school.

Okay, okay, quite a few strange things happened to me in high school. But this is a good one and affects something even more serious than losing your cable during the SuperBowl.

Yep, PMS. Pre-Murder Syndrome.

One morning, I woke to find someone's arm lying heavily over my face. This is not something you want to wake up to (you probably wouldn't want to go asleep to this, either). Anyway, I tried to brush the arm away from my face, and got really scared, because it wouldn't move.

That's because it was my own arm lying across my face!

Sometime, during the night, I must have draped my arm over my face and cut off the circulation. With thoughts of gangrene racing through my mind, I lifted the peacefully slumbering arm with the other hand. It was non-responsive, and so heavy I dropped it by accident, whacking myself on the head, nearly causing a concussion. I rubbed the arm furiously, until it tingled painfully back to life. Whew!

49

Once the worry about gangrene was eliminated, I remember reflecting about how our body works. The fact that we are mostly fluids and things work by hydraulics, levers, and other cool physics stuff, like gravity.

Anyway, some people say that a woman's period is caused by the moon's gravitational pull, much the same way it affects the oceans and causes tides. That's why they have a period once a month as the moon goes through its phases. That got me to thinking that earth women are actually pretty lucky. What would happen if we lived on Jupiter or Saturn, where there are many moons? Would they have more periods? Or if the sun, which is quite a bit denser, was closer, they might find themselves having a period every day!

Someday I'm sure doctors will figure out a cure for PMS and its resultant mood swings.

But, you know, we don't really have to wait, because, being a guy, I figured out a permanent solution.

Are you ready?

If we were to blast the moon out of existence, there would be no more periods, so no more PMS!

I'm sure at this point that you might be wondering just what force we could generate that would be enough to destroy a small planet.

Well, I have the answer for this, too.

We just ship a rocket **full of women with PMS** up to the moon!

I wouldn't give the moon much chance at surviving.

The guys of our world, being guys, would probably start a pool to guess how long the moon would last.

Um, er...

I'd like to put my money on twenty minutes right now.

Ohio Schoolboard Justice
Did you hear about the Ohio schoolgirl who was suspended for taking a Midol in school?

She was suspended, because she was caught borrowing a Midol from a friend, rather than going to the nurse, explaining her problem, having her parents contacted, ads taken out in the local newspaper with blazing yellow and black billboards, not to mention a blaring announcement on the school speaker system, along with a permanent mark added to her school records that would follow her through all of her life, including the interview she will do in the year 2012 where she meets Mark, who dazzles her with his sensitivity and poise, but how, upon learning of her PMS background, deigns to ask her out for fear of her dark side.

All rather than quietly downing an over-the-counter medication in total privacy, hoping to alleviate some of the pains and discomfort associated with being a woman.

I saw her on the news, and saw that she is a cute, slender innocent-looking girl, honor student, and everything. It staggers my mind that they came down so hard on her. It's not that I don't agree with the principle of keeping drugs out of our schools. I wholeheartedly agree with clamping down on drugs, and keeping them out of the hands of our children. I have two children in school, who are subject to the temptations to experiment that arise when hundreds of kids are crammed together without a TV to immobilize them.

But I firmly believe they should keep weapons out of schools. I try to imagine the scene that day when the girl, actually a woman, staggering through the school, armed and dangerous with PMS, the most lethal concealed weapon. At that time, this slim girl was probably the most dangerous person in Ohio, capable of disemboweling the entire front line of the Dallas Cowboys.

Heroically refusing to unleash her womanly fury, she chemically disarms herself (learn something from this, Saddam!), as her friend, also capable of the same fury, slips her a Midol. The little pill that could quell the storm inside her. She lurches to the drinking fountain, and hastily gulps the Midol, slorking water which streams unheeded down her face. This little pill somehow knows exactly what to do and where to go.

She slumps exhausted against a locker, and school authorities, who had been vigilantly maintaining a safe distance until her inner beast is contained, pounced on her and slapped her in cuffs. Muzzling her, they drag the now-helpless girl down to the principal's office to administer **Ohio School Board Justice**.

Meanwhile, down the hall, little Betsy Demont feels the first flush of PMS symptoms. The next day's *Ohio Star* chronicled the disgruntled mailman-like carnage the PMS-enraged Betsy, when unable to take a Midol, unleashed in the cafeteria.

The second page of the paper had a follow up blurb, that the first student's suspension was to take effect the beginning of the next year. Major league umpires threatened to strike unless her suspension started immediately.

(unrelated?) …

An actual edition of the *Chicago Tribune's* local police and fire report contained the following blurb:

"A 21-year-old Evergreen Park woman was arrested after she was accused of throwing a glass ashtray at a man, hitting a woman in the head, biting a man and damaging a mailbox at an apartment building on the 17300 block of South 70th Avenue on Wednesday. Maria Wilde, of Lawndale Ave. was charged with battery and criminal damage to property and released on $1000 bond. She is scheduled to appear in court Sept. 16."

(Uh, for purely self-preservation purposes, I changed her name to protect the Me. For obvious reasons, as I'm sure you can understand.)

So what's this guy's excuse…?

A thirty-four year old Hinsdale man was arrested Thursday after he was accused of hitting a Westmont police officer. He was charged with resisting arrest after he allegedly punched a police officer and struggled with other officers when they woke him from a nap on a friend's bathroom floor.

Exclamation Point

Back to the woman's period. If there's anything that's misnamed, it's this little event. At least make it an exclamation point, or something. Calling it a period is kind of like naming the biggest dinosaur ever discovered some trivial name, like Floyd. Call it something big, like an Eaticusraptorus, or something. A dignified name, lending necessary weight to something that shook the ground when it walked.

Similarly, a woman's period is more than a simple dot in a woman's life. It's a mood-altering event! Surely, we can give it a name that closer typifies the fear it inspires in men. How about calling that time of month **The Rage**? Or, since this is a tidal wave going on in a woman's body, calling it **The Wave**, or **The Tide**? Or give it varying names, depending on the severity, to allow women to adequately be able to warn their man. Call it **The Wave** if it's kind of a mellow period. A more severe once would be **The Tide**, and a real warning for the guy could be **The Tidal Wave**.

The guy should leave the country if one appears called **Tsunami.**

PMS

I know it seems I joke a lot about PMS, but I really take Pre-Murder Syndrome very seriously. It was something I didn't really run into when I was dating. These must have been the nights when my date would be 'washing her hair.' That's because she didn't want me to see the transformation that takes place as this sweet, young innocent turns into something that would frighten the burliest of men right out of his back hair.

I believe that men should have PMS too, not just to understand; but because I really think everyone goes insane once a month. Women, being the civilized half, developed PMS as an early warning system for the male half. I know PMS seems to be a drastic way to warn men, but you have to hit a guy pretty hard before he'll take a hint.

Anyway, men go nuts, too, and I don't just mean on Super Bowl Sunday. In the caveman days, a man simply went out and stabbed something to reduce his pent-up frustrations. Now that this mostly frowned upon, though some still do it, we just go ahead and jump in a car.

You know the way PMS transforms a woman? Isn't it a remarkable coincidence how much a man is transformed when he turns the ignition key in a car?

I rest my case.

Chapter 6   Guys and Aliens, er, Kids

Actually, there's very little difference between guys and kids (ask my wife). So, in a way, this is just another chapter about guy's traits.

Fuddy-duddy

When did I become a fuddy-duddy?

Seriously, it seems like just yesterday that I was on the forefront of music and television. Yeah, I was cool and trendy. I liked Pink Floyd and M*A*S*H, two very happening things. My hair was long and wild. I was a rebel. A free thinker in striped bell-bottoms.

Nowadays, I just don't get it. Everybody's rapping, wearing their hats backwards and piercing every part of their faces and anatomy. For fun they dive off bridges attached to rubber-bands and plummet skateboards down the hand-rest bars of steps.

Meanwhile, I'm a dad, a fuddy-duddy. My long hair migrated to my nose and ears, leaving behind a deserted scalp. If I want to hear a good tune, I need only step in an elevator. My kids speak in alien tongues using strange words like, "OMYGOD," and watch MTV and VH1, two alleged music stations who now only play reality television like *The Osbournes*. Meanwhile, Ozzy's music is relegated to elevators for the enjoyment of fuddy-duddies like me.

I know that some of my contemporaries have dipped into this strange new culture. Usually, they do something small, like Ashley's dad, who sports a little hoop in his left ear. Or her mom, who's got a gecko on her ankle. So they're way cooler than me, right?

Yeah, maybe. All I know is that you won't catch me dead in earrings. No tattoos, either. I also refuse to recognize the artistry of rap music, or even call rap 'music.' In my opinion, if you can't hum it, it ain't music.

But you know something? There are some people who rely on me to stay this way. To my kids, Dad should be just that, Dad. Not some hip, trendy 'dude' who paints his hair, pierces his nipples and hangs out at raves. Knowing that there is some security in their lives, they can experiment with their own individuality, all the while knowing that there is a rock in their lives. Something that they can count on to remain the same. Something that resists all change.

Me.

Anyway, I was at work one morning when my email message blipped, and I pulled up the incoming message. It was from my wife.

Smiling, I settled back to read.

The email said,

"Just wanted to give you the heads up. Your youngest informed me this morning on the drive to school that she:

    1. was listening to Pink's CD last night.

    2. kinda likes Pink's hair.

    3. is bored with her own hair.

    4. would like to dye her hair blue.

After recovering from swallowing my tongue, I informed her that:

    1. maybe if she brushed her hair a bit she would like it more.

    2. perhaps she should pick a color that doesn't appear in a box of Nerds.

    3. she would have to run it by Daddy first.

(Neener, neener, now it's your problem.)

She then told me with a pained look that I was "so mean", and that it's "just hair'."

I wasn't smiling anymore. Maybe this fuddy-duddy will just have to work a little late tonight.

I'll drive

"I'll drive."

Usually these are good words. Like on New Year's Eve when the designated driver says them. Or when your wife says them when she sees you're getting tired during a long trip. Still though, there are times when these two words are scary enough to curl your ear hair.

But when my fifteen-year old daughter, proud possessor of a brand new driver's permit, excitedly blurted them, did I panic?

No way. I'm a guy. After years of conditioning, we guys are trained not to blink. When a curve ball decides not to curve, do we blink? No way. We just fall down, and brush ourselves off. We don't blink when staring down the cat. We don't blink when the model walks around the ring between boxing rounds. We don't blink at the beach.

But when Sam volunteered to drive, I blinked.

What you don't know yet is what I haven't told you. The 'what' I haven't told you about was the time last summer when my wife and I went to the grocery store, and left Sam in charge at home. I know, I know, not a big deal, right?

But when we came out of the store, our cell phone rang. Sandy answered, and then listened intently. I could hear excited noises coming from the phone. When she calmly hung up, she announced, "There's been an accident."

Now when a guy, a father, hears, "there's been an accident," our minds, which usually run in a quiet idle, crank up the RPM's so that our brain is racing like the winner of a NASCAR race. In the space of two seconds, we can clearly imagine fifteen or more separate and distinct 'accidents' that all involve loss of limb, life or spilled beer.

Obviously, these thoughts all crossed my face, because Sandy quickly added, "nobody's hurt."

Good news here. I shot a message to my lungs telling them it was okay to get back to work.

Seems that Sam wanted to shoot some hoops in the driveway. Because she would be driving soon, I'd been letting her practice driving in our driveway. Supervised, I might add.

Anyway, my car had been parked in the driveway, and she didn't want to scratch it...ha, ha. So, she decided to pull into the garage.

Yeah, I know what you're thinking, and you're right.

She pulled into the garage, all right. All the way in. In fact, further than the garage was wont to allow. When she was pulling in, the car slowed, so she tried to give it a little goose. Unfortunately, she gave it an ostrich instead, and the car jumped forward, gently touching the back of my garage.

I wish. Actually, the car slammed into my riding lawn mower, and knocked it through the back of the garage, totaling the mower and providing unwanted ventilation for the garage.

So did I blink when Sam said she'd drive? Yeah, maybe. But that was all. Then I said, "Sure, hon, sounds great." Then, manfully, I handed over the keys.

Student Teachers

Hang-gliding? Bah, no comparison. Snake-charming? Child's play. Extreme rock-climbing? Pah-shaw!

You want excitement? Try handing your car keys to your fifteen-year old. Not only that, but then strap yourself in the passenger's seat and go along for the ride. Do you think Great America offers a ride with more thrills and spills than this? Well, Batman can just take a backseat. Even the Mafia lets you take your last drive in the safety of the trunk, with nice bags of cement to rest your head on.

Illinois has a really interesting way of teaching the next generation how to drive. Their method? Us! They have us do it! The parents! And they do it without installing brakes on the passenger's side. Jeez, who said we're qualified to do this? Every day, I see more and more evidence that the last people who should be instructing tomorrow's drivers are today's drivers. But our Secretary of State ...

Wait.. time to digress. What's it say for us that the head of Illinois' transportation system is a secretary? The highways, byways, myways, yourways, and everything else. It's not important enough for the bigwigs to handle? They have to put a secretary in charge of it? I don't mean to denigrate secretaries or anything, but how do typing, nail maintenance and phone skills qualify you to deal with potholes, passing lanes, driver examination tests and organ donor cards?

Not only that, but instead of bothering to do it himself, he delegates it even further down the line... to us. Well, if he just passes his job along to me, he can just forget about getting a card next Secretary's Day. Still though, it's good to see that our Secretary, who is a guy, isn't afraid to take on a job that people consider a woman's job. Good for him.

Anyway, when my daughter told me that she has to drive with a parent for twenty-five hours before she could qualify for her license, I thought it was a great idea. That way I could help her learn how to avoid necessary evils like blind spots and pot holes; not to mention Grand Prix's and Monte Carlos, who all treat other cars as obstacles to be conquered by bull rushes to merges and tail-gating.

So, one fine day, with a queasy stomach and shaky knees, I handed the keys for my Camry to the young woman who will eventually bear my grandchildren, and I eased into the unfamiliar passenger seat next to her. Ninety pounds worth of teen-aged hormones slid into the driver's seat, cranked the engine, and started backing confidently out of the driveway.

And then I asked, with a manful squeak, "So how many times have you driven with the instructor?"

She grinned, and said, "Oh, we don't drive with the instructors until after we do our twenty-five hours with the parents."

SKREECH!!!!!

That wasn't the car. That was my heart.

"You haven't driven!"

"No, why? Is that a problem?"

"Of course not," I whimpered "Drive on."

Rotten Eggs

The Easter Bunny was caught at our house once. After the kids had been tucked in their beds, with visions of chocolate eggs in their heads, Sandy and I were in the basement building their Easter baskets. Samantha, our elder daughter, had left a note upstairs for Mr. Bunny, who usually answered with his signature bunny prints.

With the girls safely away, we were dumping chocolate robin eggs, jellybeans, and other bunny stuff into the two baskets, when a small voice came from the bottom of the stairwell. And there she was, Samantha, staring with saucer-eyes at the baskets, "I can't sleep," she said in a scared voice. She knew instinctively something was going on that was major, major news.

Sandy shooed her back to bed, and spoke with her for awhile.

The next day, Sam sidled up to me, and in a low voice said, "Daddy, I know the truth about the Easter Bunny."

Yeah, my ears were showing.

With a sad sigh, I said, "Oh, what about him?" (figuring I'd have to bind her to confidentiality about her little sister, Lauren).

Then, looking around, she whispered, "I know you and Mommy help the Easter Bunny by putting everything but the chocolate bunny in the baskets." She then added, helpfully, with a secret smile, "But don't worry, I won't tell Lauren."

Good save, Sandy

Still, it made me wonder about the wisdom of deceiving our children about that Santa dude, storks and a rabbit that leaves eggs.

I'm afraid that when they learn the truth, they'll wonder what else we've lied to them about. Will they doubt stories of

God too, thinking these are just other stories meant to give to them the gift of magic?

I took the kids to Chuckie Cheese (Motto: "We'll be happy to just vacuum out your wallet for you."), and Sam came up and said, "Guess what? I just heard a couple Mom's trying out that 'C'mon, or we'll leave you,' thing with their kids."

She clearly, and rightly, knew that this was a deception. I try, as hard as I can, to keep my word to my kids. If I promise them ice cream for cleaning the family room, they get it. If I'm angry, and count 'One, Two, …" they know not to let me hit Three.

But I'm not, I know it, always completely honest with them.

Am I the only one bothered by all of this?

God's Favorite Color

Once I had kids I had to prepare myself to try to answer questions they ask in a way that will keep their heads from exploding. For example, a common 'kid' question is, "Why is the grass green?"

Everybody knows that grass is actually every color **except** green! What happens is that when white light rays, which are a composite of every color (a prism shows you this), hit a blade of grass, the grass absorbs all of the colors except green, which bounces back to your eyes. So basically you are just seeing the reject color. I could continue my explanation by informing them that your eyes actually invert the image and your brain interprets the image upside down.

Somehow it's a lot easier to respond, "Because God likes green."

...

There are number of great things about having kids, but here are some of the lesser appreciated:

- You don't look silly when you stop the Good Humor ice cream truck.

- It's okay to browse the toy aisle.
- Somebody's always willing to play "Sorry."
- You won't jeopardize your macho image if you're seen at a Disney movie.
- Hands will always add candy to your cart, so you don't have to worry about the temptation.
- You get to buy Play Station.
- There's somebody to teach you how to get through a game on Play Station.

Supercalifragilisticexpialidocious
Please don't think I'm weird here (too late, huh?), but I simply want to use the next two words in one sentence:
(are you ready?)
Here goes ...
The only word bigger than antidisestablishmentarianism, is the word supercalifragilisticexpialidocious, which I heard while trying to pick up a cockney accent; and the only thing they have in common, besides being long words, is that neither makes it through my spell check without angry red squiggly lines underneath like the kind that show up when you type anything an attorney wrote, because they don't know how to spell, so they just make up words and pass laws that make their new words legal like when they make really, really, long convoluted sentences that contain a whole bunch of legalese to confuse any laymen, who are defined as anyone who cannot read attorney-speak without falling into a coma wherein their attorney will bill them three hundred dollars an hour while they draw up powers of attorney and stuff like that.

Hand-Marking
I'm ambidextrous, in my case this means that I do things equally poorly with either hand. No one else in my family is as confused or has to make the same choice when it comes to writing, eating, throwing or picking their noses. The root for my confusion, I'm positive, comes from the fact that it took me an

awfully long time to figure out the difference between my right and left hands.

I'm sure that if I would have had cheat sheets, or had my hands marked with "L" and "R" I'd at least use the correct hand, even though I might be using the wrong fork at classy dinner joints.

Well, guess what? Our hands **are** marked! Sandy used a very clever way to teach our kids the difference between their right and left hands. She showed them that if you hold your left hand out in front of you, looking at the top of your hand, and stretch your thumb perpendicularly with your hand, your forefinger and thumb make the "L" shape.

I never knew this!

This is one of the many things I love about having children. Not only do I get to relive parts of my childhood (like scarfing cotton candy), but I also get a second chance to learn things I never knew and wouldn't normally get a chance to think about. (Chuck, Chuck bo buck, banana fanna fo f....., shame on you if you finish this!!)

Most people don't know that boys actually learn to write earlier than girls do. You'd think girls would learn earlier, since they actually use both sides of their brain. But think about it, boys are born with their first writing instrument!

Women, ask your man if he ever wrote his name in the snow (you know what I mean!). While girls are out in the first snowfall making snow angels, and catching flakes on their tongues; boys are out carving their names in yellow in the snow, using Koolaid for ammo.

Cartoons
Another nice thing about having children is that I have a good excuse to watch cartoons. Hey, I'm just bonding, O.K.?! So what if there isn't always a child in the room? Anyway, I noticed that

most cartoon stars are wardrobe-challenged. George Jetson wears a white shirt and blue slacks every day! And what's with the white shoes?

Charlie Brown has just one shirt, a brown one with the black zigzag stripe, or a whole closet of them. Fred and Wilma always wear the same leopard spot and white dress, respectively. And why can't Superman try purple and black, or maybe green and yellow? Is he afraid no one will recognize him?

For a while, I resented the fact that Loonytoons and Hanna Barbara have so little respect for our children's ability to recognize cartoon characters from day to day, that they had to dress them in the same clothes show after show after show. Then I figured out why. They all wear the same clothes, because, with only three fingers, they can't manage buttons very well.

Yesterday, I had to sign something, so I held my hands out in front of me, so I could figure out which one to write with. (Picture this, now, OK?) I peered intently at the palms of both hands, and shifted both thumbs perpendicular to my index fingers. Then I saw the "L" made by my index finger and thumb on my non-ring hand. So I knew this was my left hand. I'm sure glad I learned this little trick!

Word Play
Huh?

It turns out that I'm wrong about something.

This can't be true, you say, right?

Because it's obvious that I'm just about as knowledgeable and good-looking as it is possible to be. Even more, I'm balding, a manly man of men.

I know you're thinking this.

Si?

Well, out with it. Here goes...

I was wrong when I said that the longest word in the English language was 'supercalifragilisticexpialidocious.' And it's not even 'antidisestablishmentarianism.'

Neither of these words even come close to the longest word.

So all you kids who learned how to spell antidisestablishmentarianism wasted your time!

Ha! Ha! Ha!

Especially the showoffs who actually learned it backwards.

The longest word, and I'm serious as a toenail clipping, is ...

Not 'floccinaucinihilipilification.'

And it's not, 'homework.'

Or 'taxes.'

Or 'infinity.'

It's, ...

(is the suspense killing you?)

Here goes...

No, really, here it goes, for real...

Right now...

.....**pneumonoultramicroscopicsilicovolcanoconiosis!!!!!**

Boo Yah! Now that's a word, huh?

Now don't you go rushing for your Webster's, because you're not going to find it there. You know why?

Because it's a medical word, made up by doctors. An alien almost-human species, closely related to lawyers and paleontologists, best known for abusing our language, and whacking divots out at the golf course with their stock options.

I know, I know. You doubt my seriousness. How can a word that simply combines pneumonia, mon, ultra, microscopic, silly, volcano, cone, I and sis, be the longest word in the language?

I don't know! I didn't do it! So leave me alone.

But let's think about it.

Hmmm.

Maybe it's about someone from the Caribbean who goes to Washington to visit his sister, and on a silly whim, climbs to the cone of a volcano whereas an ultra-mean microscopic microbe with an identity crisis gives him a nasty case of pneumonia.

Nope, that's not it.

65

For those of you who care, you'll find that it is a lung disease caused by inhaling very fine silia dust, or by sharing an elevator with an attorney.

So all you kids know what's next, don't ya?

Yep, start memorizing!

Needles

One of the scariest thoughts about getting married was my fear of the blood test. Being naïve back then, I hadn't yet learned about PMS, so I was to learn later just how piddly the blood test would be in comparison. And believe me, after years of cleaning dog barf, watching kids brought into the world, and fending off telemarketers, I have developed a warrior's resistance to blood and guts. But little did I suspect my daughter Lauren of the same fortitude.

When she was four years old, we took her in for her pre-school physicals, and learned she was anemic. She was put on iron tablets, but when she was tested again, her anemia was even worse. The doctor wasn't concerned yet, because she was zipping around without any of the scary symptoms anemia sometimes indicates. Still though, we were told we'd have to bring her to the hospital for some blood work.

A couple years before, when she was just under two, she had blood taken, and they had trouble finding a vein. They pricked her left arm three times, her right arm twice, and both feet before they finally found a vein. She was a crying, screaming mess of snot and tears. We were sweating and panicking, and her older sister was valiantly trying to entertain her with goofy faces and noises.

With this horrible precedent, we put off going in for her new test for almost two months. Then, one day at work, one of my co-workers told about her little four-year old niece, who contracted leukemia. This got my attention, and the next day we took Lauren in.

We told her what was going to happen, and promised her anything from *Toys R Us* when we were done. We reassured her we'd be there the whole time, and not let any telemarketers in the room.

When we got there, we waited in the waiting room (uh, yeah, of course), and Lauren was playing and climbing and crawling and making friends. When the nurse called her name, we took her hand, and, still encouraging her, took her in the back to a little chair with arms similar to the old chair-desks back in grade school. I squished into the chair, and Lauren sat on my lap. The two cheerful nurses were being that fake cheerful and tied a rubber strand around her arm. One of them started prodding experimentally at her arm, and told the other she couldn't find a very good vein. I started sweating at this point, but fortunately they found a good one on her other arm.

They inserted the needle, and Lauren watched with fascinated interest as they drew three whole vials of her blood. The only visible sign of nervousness or discomfort she showed the whole time, was when she started shaking her foot slightly. She never said a word, until they were done and asked her if she wanted a Yogi Bear or Jetsons band-aid.

I kept waiting for a delayed, tearful explosion as they offered her a sucker for being so good. She gravely thanked them for the sucker, and asked if she could have another for her sister. We took her hand, and as we were walking out, Sandy and I thanked the nurses for their tenderness and concern.

Then, and I swear I'm not kidding, Lauren piped up and said, "Thanks a lot! And thanks for the shot!"

Poem

Here's a poem by my daughter Samantha, when she was thirteen:

> I wake up and hear distant caroling,
> The sweet smell of fresh-baked gingerbread
> > Cookies floats into my room.
> My sister comes running in,
> Her face lit up and a huge toothy smile.
> > I smile as well, as I leap out of bed
> > > And we run down the dark hall
> > > > Jackpot!
> There, under the calm, glistening, proud tree are my prizes
> Presents galore, neatly stacked under the tree,
> > waiting to be opened.
> My parents come out with tired faces,
> > But they smile when they see us ripping through the presents joyfully.
> > > We all exchange thank you's, and agree it has been a great Christmas.

Tweety

I don't mean to spark a debate or anything, but one of the deep, philosophical questions that has baffled pundits and deep thinkers for decades is, and I'm not being homophobic or anything, when I ask, "Is Tweety a boy or a girl?"

Gotcha, didn't I?

You have no clue, do you? And you probably haven't even thought about it, have you? Good thing you have me around to wonder about those things that you're too busy to wonder about, huh?.

So here's Tweety, hanging around with an umbrella-wielding maniac who's pretending to be an old lady, when we know she's actually something out of the *Star Wars* cast. Meanwhile, Tweety's got those long eyelashes, and enjoys swinging back and forth on his/her swing.

Well, I've gone behind this simple deception, and figured out the answer. It has to do with the way Tweety sings, and what kind of music I prefer.

A little background. If you ask me who my favorite singing groups are, I'm going to give you a macho answer, like Pearl Jam, Stone Temple Pilots and Dave Matthews. But what you don't know, and what I'm not going to admit, especially in writing, is that really the singers I listen to are more likely to come from the Lilith Fair, like Sarah McLachlan, Fiona Apple, Enya, Dido and Cheryl Crow. Well, I really do like Dave Matthews, but that's an exception.

Where was I going with this? Oh yeah. Anyway, it seems that I secretly (don't tell anyone) really prefer women singers.

But I don't like Tweety.

At all.

I'm always rooting for Sylvester to chomp the obnoxious avian. And I don't like the way he sings. So there we have it. Since I don't like the way he sings, …. he's a he.

[warning: if you object to the word 'poop,' do not read the following section. My wife hates this whole paragraph, because of the word 'poop.' So if you prefer not to see the word 'poop,' which is a normal every day human function, just skip down to the next section, where you will not see the word 'poop.']

Poop

Why is poop brown? When my little one Lauren was a toddler, I'd watch her scarf down red, purple, green, and yellow stuff, wash them down with blue, white, orange and other the other Kool-aid colors; and a little later it all comes back out, but minus the colors.

Thanks to Kool-aid, Scarfers Candy Company, and other wholesales of colored food/waste products, we consume rainbows of colors every day, and just end up pooping out a non-varying brown sludge instead. I experimented one week with my dog, who will eat anything. He got orange melons one day, yellow bananas the next, green eggs for another and, sure enough, it came out brown. So I tried *Crayolas*, a dog-delicacy, wondering if we'd get pretty poop; and, sure enough, his gastric system recognized, unlike his mouth, that *Crayolas* aren't food. They passed right through, looking like colored candy chips in chocolate cookie rolls.

After this intense scientific study, I developed the theory that we all have rainbows trapped in us, and the newly-discovered lint creature comes to feed on the rainbows every day, slurping quietly through our bellybuttons.

Little Girls

When my girls were little, they learned just how to twist me around their candy-stained little fingers. I used to get out of work half an hour before my wife had to be at her part-time job. There was no time for me to get home before she had to leave, so we would meet midway. Our girls were too young to leave at home with candy in the house, so Sandy would pack them in the van and bring them along with her.

One day, when we met, Samantha came up to me and earnestly blurted, "Daddy, I know you're really hungry when you get out of work. And it's okay if you say 'no,' but there's a little knapsack the older girls are wearing, and it's really cool." Without pausing, she continued, "And Mommy said you'd be really hungry, so I made this sandwich for you, and ... these snacks... and ....will you get one for me??"

All this planning and consideration floored me. I looked at Sandy, and saw she was quietly smirking. She shouldn't have been, because everything she made that night was spent getting the knapsack, a pair of shoes for each of the girls, some Disney stuff, and dinner for the girls and me at Chi Chi's.

Barbie

Another time, when the kids were little, we bonded together with cartoons and Cheetos, and tuned in to, yes, Looney-Toons. Ah, the first show up was the Pink Panther, one of my favorites from the silent movies, along with Charlie Chaplin.

Pink was putting up a sign that said, "No Trespassing Allowed" on a snowy hill. But somehow, the 'No' snaps off, and before you can blink, a skier blasts through, knocking Pink on his tail. Peter Sellers, I mean, the Pink Panther, leaps to his feet, and shouts, "Hey, no trespassing!!"

....Huh?

What did I just write? The Pink Panther can talk?!! That can't be!

Frantically, I flipped through the channels over the kids' outraged protestations, and found another cartoon. Good old Bugs.

Wait a minute! He's colored a garish green. And that's not Mel Blanc! Bugs doesn't even sound like Bugs! Not even close.

Then, two ducks went lisping onto the screen, who look a little like Daffy, and sound maybe like the famous duck, but they're red!! What's going on here?!?! What are they doing to our classic cartoons??

Deeply concerned, I roamed, searching for in vain for what I remember from my childhood. I stopped for a moment on "The New Adventures of Johnny Quest." Who were these kids pretending to be Johhny and Haji (beats me how to spell it)? "The Superfriends" had Batman and Robin, Flash, Green Lantern, Hawkman, Wonder Woman, and a couple new ones I never heard of. Superman was in this show too.

I must digress here, for I read probably every early Superman issue. I realize they've developed him more since then, with his death, his marriage to Lois and gay affair with Jimmy Olsen (just kidding, though I wonder sometimes about Jimmy), and making him pregnant (no, wait, that was Arnold Schwartzeneger).

Back when I was reading Superman, I was a kid, with a vocabulary and occasional entire conversations consisting of burps and farts. So it was just kind of normal to wonder about Superman's natural functions. What do you think a Superman sneeze would do? And did you ever see him eat or drink? And what happens when he pees? I imagined a urinal just blasting through the bathroom wall, with Superman standing there, the front of his tights pulled down, and his Super-hood exposed. And I don't know about you, but I wouldn't want to near him after a plate of franks and beans.

Sorry, I got sidetracked. Back to the morning with my kids and the cartoons.

Unable to accept this blatant rewriting of all the cartoons that got me to the stage of puberty, I turned off the TV, and took the kids out for some air, and other stuff at a nearby store.

As always, they put the toy sections in the front as a parent-trap, so my kids physically overpowered me, and dragged my semi-conscious body into the toy section. Being girls, they swept right on by the cool boy toys, right to the Barbie isle. That's right, a whole isle totally devoted to Barbie. And not just to Barbie accessories, that's another two whole isles. The isle they took me to had just Barbie. Beach Party Barbie, Malibu Barbie, Baywatch Barbie, Congresswoman Barbie, Shopping Barbie, with her daughter Kellie.

Wait, Barbie has a daughter?

I broke the vice grips the two tiny bodies had on me, and peered intently at Shopping Barbie for a better look.

Yep, sure enough, she has a daughter now. I'm sure it's not by Ken, who is gay, of course. Back when I was a kid, my G.I. Joe tortured this admission out of him. We found he had a boyfriend named Jimmy (Hmmmm).

Barbie, of course, still looks great. Obviously, after having her baby, she went on a stringent workout regimen with Cindy Crawford. I checked her out, admiring the flawless figure, the perfect, nipple-less bosom, the ... WAIT!! THIS IS A FAKE!! BARBIE DIDN'T HAVE A KID!! THIS IS A FRAUD!!

How do I know this?

No stretch marks.

Graduation

A time for caps, gowns, partying. An end to an era.

One of the women at work is taking a day off for graduation. Seems her daughter is graduating from pre-school.

Graduating?

Pre-school?

Ha! Ha! Ha! Ha! Ha!

You don't **graduate** from pre-school!

For that matter, you don't graduate from grade school or junior high school either.

You finish them. Complete them. You haven't graduated. There were no final exams.

Graduated means you don't have to go to school any more.

Imagine going to your doctor's office, and there, next to a medical degree from University of Michigan, is a diploma from Paw Paw Elementary School? You think this is on her resume?

Yeah, right.

And you look more carefully, and you see yet another diploma, pink, decorated with little flowers and kitty cats, where you learn that she was the Valedictorian from Little Tots Pre-School, where she maintained a GPA of 4.0, having excelled at napping, coloring and eating milk and cookies, a habit she still struggles with to this day.

Sour grapes, you ask?

You probably figured it out. I didn't go to kindergarten or pre-school.

To this day, that's why I lack in socialization skills.

Chapter 7 Guys and SEX

If you're a guy, you probably saw this in the Table of Contents and turned here first.

Ha! Ha! Ha! The joke's on you! Sorry, no pictures. No Penthouse Forum stuff.

I could do a whole book on Guys and Sex, since, outside of Monday Night Football, nothing else interests a guy so much as does sex.

Once he's married, sex becomes just a memory, or something that comes up when your daughter asks if her pet rabbit is a boy or a girl, and you peer carefully under its tail. And as far as your daughter and the 'sex talk', that's better left to your wife to explain.

Anyway, since I'm married, sex is just a memory, and my memory isn't that good. So I'm not going to spend much time on sex.

Sorry, guys.

Considerable Cleavage

(Published in the Chicago Tribune Sunday, November 30, 2003)

I was giving a seminar one time, and during a break a very attractive woman touched my sleeve, and said, "Hi, Norm, how are you doing?"

This caused a mild dilemma, for I had no clue who she was.

Did I mention that she was good looking? Yeah, I thought I did. But what I didn't mention is that we were all wearing nametags. Nametags are that wonderful invention someone came up with to try to prevent social embarrassment when a group of people who meet infrequently, or for the first time, get together. It's supposed to **reduce** clumsy introductions. So I shouldn't have a problem, right? Just check out the nametag, run the name through the old memory banks, and *voila*, no problem.

I mentioned that she was wearing a dress, right?

With cleavage?

And not just cleavage, we're talking **Considerable Cleavage**.

I noticed this, but only because I'm a guy. So it's not my fault.

But even worse, do you know where her nametag was? Yep, right on her bosom, both near to and too near, the ravine of wonders. So my mind was racing, trying to figure out how to check out her name tag, without making it look like I was drinking in an eyeful of cleavage for a cheap thrill.

I stammered out an answer, wondering where the heck she knew me from, and also wondering how I could direct her attention somewhere else for a second, so that I could take a quick look at her nametag.

Then I was saved. Another acquaintance showed up, and the woman's attention flickered to him for a second. Unlike mine, his eyes were firmly locked on her bosom as he approached, though I'm sure it was for innocent reasons. Did I mention it was considerable cleavage?

So I took advantage of the distraction, and took a quick peek at her chest. My thoughts were pure. But, without will, … my …eyes …. were ….drawn ….irresistibly …. to … her ….well, you know.

Her eyes swung back to me, and mine guiltily sucked back into the sockets. Damn! I still didn't know who she was.

Now my acquaintance was looking at me, an expectant look on his face. And so was she. And I realized to my horror why. They didn't know each other, and were waiting for me to introduce them to each other! My brain retreated into the safety of record-lock, and all of a sudden, I couldn't remember his name! For that matter, I couldn't even remember my own name.

Total mental breakdown!

That one peek drove everything out of my mind, except Cleavage. And there was simply so much of that, there just wasn't room for anything else.

I was saved by the bell, because right then we were called back into the seminar. Somehow, my mind snapped back into focus in time for me to speak intelligently.

But I still never got over my 'some-timers disease' regarding the woman's name, and I haven't seen her cleavage, um face, since.

That's about it for sex. Get thee to a magazine if you want anything else.

Chapter 8   Guys are ani.. oops, guys and animals

Guys relate closely to animals. Maybe a little too close, in some cases.

The Freedom to Poop

There are those that say I shouldn't do it (They're probably right.)

Anyway, I was on one end of a leash. There was a basset hound on the other end, sniffing around for the best place to poop. This process can take several minutes, so I found myself with time to think.

That's the thing I shouldn't be doing. Not pooping... thinking.

Because when you're at one end of a leash, with the mighty Pooping Machine at the other, your mind starts wandering, since you don't really want to watch what's going on with the dog.

I wondered that we've lost one of our most important freedoms. That freedom?

The freedom to evacuate our waste.

Hold on! Don't go away! Sheesh. It's a normal human function. It's okay to talk about it!

Think about it. Back in the frontier days, if you had to go, you went behind a bush, did your business, wiped with whatever leaves were available, prayed that they weren't poison ivy, and kicked dirt over the whole thing.

Think you could get away with this now?

Nope. Nowadays we have to rely on the friendly folks at McDonalds.

Aw, c'mon. Don't tell me you've never done it.

You're driving around, clutching a Big Gulp in your lap since it won't fit in your cup holder, and Mother Nature calls.

Trouble is, you can't answer the old-fashioned nature way. You have to find a restroom.

So where do you go?

Well, it's against the law to urinate or defecate in public, right? So wouldn't you think our lawmakers would put up all kinds of nice restrooms for us, paid for with our tax dollars? Yeah, right, they're too busy raising taxes. And sure, you can find the occasional public restroom out on the freeways. But how good are these going to do you if you're not on the freeway?

Nope, you're forced to rely on the hospitality of strangers, like McDonalds.

So you pull up to McDonald's, your bladder screaming obscenities at you for waiting so long, and you rush into the Mc-restroom, do your business, and rush back to your car, ... without even stopping to buy a Big Mac!!

You expect the restroom to be clean. Paid for by McDonalds. There'd better be toilet paper, right? Paid for by McDonalds. Soap? (Well, for most people.) Paid for by McDonalds. Heated? Brrrr. Yep, gots to be heated. Paid for by McDonalds. Condoms? Well, maybe not at McDonalds, but you sure expect gas stations to provide this necessary vending service.

You get the point.

I don't feel guilty about it. I always rationalize that I give McDonalds quite a bit of business every year, so it's okay that I use their Mc-restrooms whenever I need to, whether I'm in for chicken nuggets or not.

Still, though, it's a strange kind of entitlement, isn't it?

Yup.

You know. My dog goes poop about three times a day.

Lots of time to think.

I'm sure you appreciate this, right?

Fat Cat

I like animals and have owned both cats and dogs. Right now I own a stupid basset (this is itself an oxymoron) that my children named Buster. This is one of the better names they have come up with when we give them the privilege. My older daughter, Samantha, when she was young, once got a toy giraffe from the gift shop at Brookfield Zoo and named it 'Haack' (like a big wad of spit). She was around four at the time, and also christened her doll 'Baby Ka Ka' (like poop).

Anyway, having owned both kinds of animals I feel I'm entitled to make a few generalizations. First, contrary to public opinion, cats are more polite than dogs. Just look how they eat. When a dog eats, spit, slobber and food fly in every direction. Then, when they're done gobbling, they nose around, Hoovering up bits of food, spittle, and pushing the bowl around hoping, I guess, to be in position when more food falls from the sky.

Before he got Junkfooditis, which earned us a stern look from the vet, we used to mix a dash of people-food in Buster's dinner. But if we forgot, he'd go on food strike for up to twenty seconds. A cat will go on food strike too, but is much more refined about it. It simply goes off and stalks away to go kill its own dinner.

Not Buster though, he gives you the same look an Italian gives you when you serve spaghetti without meatballs, "Whatsa matta, no meatballs?," and then noses around to see where you put his real dinner.

And I gotta say something here, something so gross you may have to turn your head. My dog eats poop! Did you hear me? Poop!!!!

EEEUUUUUCCCCCHHHHHKKK!!!!!

And not just any poop. Cat poop! That stuff that comes from the wrong end of a feline! Not that you'd want anything from the other end.

The kids talked me into getting our cat, with one of the main cornerstones of their argument being that **Dad Would Not Have To Do Anything To Take Care Of The Cat!** No scooping litter, no cleaning hocked up hairballs, no feeding. Nothing. No care, whatsoever. I'm scot-free.

Yeah, right. And the Easter Bunny will be leaving some Dave Matthews tickets in my basket this year.

This agreement held for about a week until everybody discovered that used litter smells like chlorine. And since I'm the swimmer in the family, they figured, well, it just seemed right that I do it.

Then our cat got fat, so he's on a restricted diet, which makes him the round, mound of cranky cat.

So in the morning, after an actual night without eating, he's like a teenager on pizza-deprivation.

And whoever steps in the kitchen first runs into one angry, hungry cat.

Guess who that would be?

With every single step, a fuzzy, plump torpedo zigzags in front of me, frantically trying to remind me that **the cat must be fed**.

This lasts until the moment food appears in his bowl. And I stagger off into the bathroom amid the frantic crunching sound of Purina salmon and eggs-flavored cat food.

Where was I leading with all this?

Oh, yeah.

When I change the litter, Buster watches with an intent look on his face. Surely he's just keeping me company, right? Yeah sure. This dog is a raging mass of impulse and instinct. The impulse to eat, and the instinct to eat. The only things he does between eating, is wishing he was eating, dreaming of eating, and pooping out what he ate.

So one day I come across a basset butt sticking out of the closet with the litter box, and I hear crunching on the business end of the dog.

"Get out of there, you stupid dog," I scream at him.

And the butt backs out hastily. And I'm looking him in the face.

Floppy ears, droopy eyes, folds of skin.

And something brown hanging out of his mouth, with little pieces of cat litter stuck on it, like sprinkles.

Gross!

That dog is never going to lick me again!!!

Hotdogging

Let's spend a few minutes on my stench, meaning, of course, my dog Buster. He's a basset hound, possessing the many fine qualities indigenous to bassets, like an incredibly keen sense of smell, second only to bloodhounds and pregnant women; and jaw strength second only to pit bulls and gum-chewing little girls.

When it comes to food, he can be a vicious beast, capable of a truly fearsome power beg. And he's been known to attack young toddlers bearing food, by leaping (in a truly graceless exhibition of clumsiness done totally on purpose to make it appear an accident) in front of them, tripping, and snatching whatever kid-slimed mash of food is clutched in their grimy hands, looking to smear on anything non-Scotch-guarded.

And I gotta tell you, it drives me nuts when I'm out walking him, and some kid comes running up, saying, "Oh look! It's one of those hotdog dogs."

Of course he isn't! If he was, I'd be throwing up.

Bassets are not the 'hotdog' dogs! The little 'hotdog' dogs are dachshunds, not bassets! Bassets are much larger, capable of squashing a dachshund with their aroma alone.

And they aren't even related. Bassets were bred from bloodhounds in France hundreds of years ago. Dachshunds were bred from, well..., um..., hotdogs, of course.

When we were out, trying to decide what kind of dog to buy, I sold Sandy on the idea of bassets. I grew up with a basset, so based on first hand experience, I knew that they are the friendliest dogs, witness that Cleo (my dog) never bit either my brother Jim or me, even though she was often the unwilling subject of many scientific experiments.

What I didn't remember, or maybe it had been somehow erased, was the stink. Hound dogs stink. They can build up a stench in a week that any self-respecting skunk would be proud to own. This stink builds up until it literally becomes a physical presence. Fortunately, though, little blocks of basset stink come in handy for a number of things around the house, like propping open doors, tripping burglars, and little slices can even be sliced off it and used for mulch.

I guess I just never noticed how bad Cleo smelled. Maybe because I stunk too. I think stink is part of the fertilizer to little boy growth. That's why they like burritos and chilidogs.

A boy's craving for food that adds to his odor is much like what a pregnant women gets for pickles (and I still have no idea why pregnant women are attracted to pickles. There are many more effective weapons available to use against the selfish bastards who got them this way. Ask Loretta Cutitt, um, uh, Bobbitt).

Well, anyway, I neglected to tell Sandy about what a hound dog smells like, a crime for which I am continuously found guilty. For example, Sandy and I are laying around watching the movie, *Enormous*, starring Tom Hanks. Buster, who had been lying in deep slumber (one of the more frequent basset positions) on the other side of the house, was suddenly roused by the one molecule of popcorn smell that accidentally wandered near his nose.

He comes nosing around, seeking to Hoover up whatever popcorn that tumbles down my shirt. And there's usually a lot, because when I eat popcorn, the whole object is to stuff as much as I can into my mouth. While this efficient technique keeps me from having to continuously dip my hand in the bowl, it also creates a surplus that Buster feels is his charge to remedy.

So he comes, sniffing around, his stench following at a discreet distance. Sandy's attention is on the movie, until the stench wafts near her, and then she'll growl, "Buster, YOU STINK!"

Normally, I wouldn't have a problem with this, but she isn't yelling this to Buster. She's looking right at me, with an accusatory glare, because it's my fault we didn't buy a poodle, which is a lot smarter and better smelling than a basset, primarily because poodles are really descended from steel wool.

Garbage Cat

A cat is raiding our garbage can on garbage day. Last night I opened our kitchen trash bag and dumped in a mostly picked-over chicken skeleton in the bag. I carried the full trash bag out to the outside trashcan, twirled the bag to secure it, and dumped it upside down into the trashcan. This morning, when I was taking the can to the road, I noticed all my neighbors' trashcans were knocked over, with garbage spilled all over. Some dogs had gotten into them.

I looked at my untouched can with disbelief, and then noticed something. The white bag that held our kitchen trash was no longer in the bag! And the chicken carcass was gone! Nothing else was disturbed, and the trash sat as neatly in the can as trash is inclined to do.

All I could figure was that some cat developed an opposable thumb, hopped into the can, grabbed the chicken, considerately dumped the trash back into the can, fought off marauding canines, put the chicken skeleton back into the kitchen bag, slung it over its shoulder, and leaped back out of the can to go daintily pick over the bones at its leisure.

See? You just won't see a dog being this considerate.

The Dog Messiah

When I was in high school, we had three dogs. Patsy (some kind of setter), Cleo (yeah, a basset), and another setter that I won't name (Misty) to protect her identity from the hordes that would descend on her if they knew this story.

This third dog was a hunter, and was kept in an enclosed chain link kennel. She was closely supervised in her daily romps in the neighboring field, and never once escaped. Little did we realize that we were going to witness a miracle. She was going to be chosen to be the mother of the dog-Messiah.

Yes, there was an immaculate conception in a house on Whiskey Run Road in Mattawan, Michigan in 1976.

The dog-God came, escorted by His dog-angels, and conceived with our virgin pedigreed dog, as she was locked securely in her kennel. Months later, on a snowy Michigan evening, the dog-Messiah was brought onto this earth to accept the sins of those dogs that get into my neighbors' trashcans.

Three wise raccoons traveled from Allegan County, bearing gifts of flea powder, chew toys, and Purina Puppy Chow. The Little Drummer woodpecker played his heart out for Him, and a beautiful shining star blazed through the snowfall.

We never learned which of the squirming puppies was the Messiah-pup, but we felt blessed just to be a part of this wonderful miracle. We thought of keeping one of the puppies in hopes we might pick the Blessed One. But upon further reflection, we decided we didn't want to clean up all the dog poop from the hordes that would come to seek His wisdom.

And we really didn't want any dog of ours to be nailed up on a cross.

Sharks

I saw an interesting show on the *Discovery* channel one night. It was called "Animal Cannibals," and some of the more interesting footage showed beetles, squirrels, mice and monkeys going off on truly gross cannibalistic rages reminiscent of Congressmen eating limp cabbage.

Well, the beetles weren't really gross, because, for some reason, I view insects something like little robots; so when beetles start tearing each other apart, it looks like *Battlebots* or something.

ATT

Anyway, one of the best features of the show was the sand tiger shark, the female of which has two uterus'! Or should this be uteri? (I don't use this word in the plural very often) What happens with the sand tiger shark is she conceives many eggs in each uterus, with each of the two uteri remaining separate from each other. When the baby sharklings are hatched within her, they immediately start devouring the other eggs and hatchlings. Usually, they eat all, if not most, of their brethren, so when the female finally conceives what comes out are two of the biggest, meanest SOB's in the bath tub.

I think herein lies the answer to controlling shark attacks. My studies are incomplete so far, but I'm willing to bet that most shark attacks are by female sharks suffering the rages of **double-PMS**, caused by having two uteri!!!

So, if we want to control shark attacks, we simply have to find a way to genetically alter sharks, so they only have a single uterus. We could develop a while new species of friendly sharks, who can be toothy friends of ours, like Flipper.

We could reverse this genetic technique, and create female humans with two uteri, for the purpose of creating a 'super soldier' army. Imagine a force of double-strength, PMS-enraged women, racing across a field to tangle with a group of, say, fanatical terrorists. If I were a terrorist, and I saw a line of raging PMS-women charging me, fresh from their mission of destroying the moon, I'd tuck my stupid terrorist tail under my cowardly butt, and go yiping away to the nearest Denny's restaurant, where I'd be found cowering and whimpering in a storage closet.

Crabby

Walt Disney productions screwed up when they made the classic cartoon movie, *The Little Mermaid*. Unfortunately, the screw-up was with my favorite character, Sebastian the crab. First of all, crabs don't turn red until **after** they are cooked! Next, crabs don't swim with forward movements, they go sideways.

This, of course, got me thinking. I wonder if there are left-handed and right-handed crabs. Do they all swim from left to right, or right to left? Can a crab go one direction, and then reverse direction? This made me realize there're a lot of things that the encyclopedia doesn't say about crabs.

Like, did you know they are the pop-top of the animal kingdom? In order to eat a crab, you turn it over and you'll see a tab on the bottom similar to the tabs on old soft drink cans. You pull the tab up, reach your finger under the shell at the back, and pull up. The whole top of the crab pulls right off.

Keeping an eye out to make sure King Triton doesn't prick you with his prong for killing his buddy, Sebastian, you scoop the yellow 'mustard' out of the middle of the crab, pull off the lungs, and *voila*, start picking out the meat.

I'm pretty interested in this lungs thing, too. Crabs, like Sebastian, can survive on land for quite a while and many crabs, like fiddler crabs, come to shore to feed. So they are one of the few animals that are as comfortable on land as they are in the water. If we could figure this out, we could prevent overpopulation by settling at the bottom of the seas. And maybe we could reopen Atlantis, too.

I was reading Dave Barry once, yeah, he's funny again, and in one of his books, he was fending off a sex-crazed crab that thought he (Dave) was after his (the crab) woman, so I started wondering about the sex habits of crabs.

One thing nature shows don't dwell on much, is sex in the animal kingdom. But once, I saw a show about crabs, and they were showing two (dos) of them mating. The male crab was caressing the female with his big claw, and she was showing signs of liking this, even though no way could she feel this through her shell. They came to a rabbit, er, rapid conclusion, and I realized I didn't see or learn anything. How, exactly, did he fertilize her? I realized that when I eat crabs, nowhere do I see anything remotely resembling a male, ….um ….organ.

I promise I'm not being a pervert if I say I'm curious how two animals resembling, in every way, tin cans, actually perform sex. Do you think you could have sex while wearing a suit of armor?

This got me thinking about which animals I've seen having sex and which would be interesting to see. I'm still not being perverted!! I'm just curious. Anyway, I've seen horses, dogs, flies (while flying too!), birds (this was a mystery until I saw it), snakes (this was truly gross) and even whales (I was impressed). I haven't seen armadillos, ostriches, porcupines, giraffes, and penguins, but I think we all would like to.

However, I have no interest in the sex habits of rats and telemarketers. Shut up! There is a difference, however minute.

So remember, if you ever run into the crab Sebastian, you can go ahead and eat him, because he's already cooked.

Got Milk?

Like you, I share a deep concern about cows and this whole flatulence thing. Think about it. Every day millions of cows crunch up grass, process it through four stomachs - yes, four stomachs! - and fart and belch methane into the atmosphere in volumes that put our colleges' frat houses to shame.

Still though, those alarmists who think there is another Ice Age in our future can rest easy knowing that a thick cloud of methane blankets our friendly little planet, keeping it warm and snuggly, if maybe a little stinky.

So that got me doing a little thinking about the whole mad cow thing and, frankly, I just don't get it. What are cows so angry about? Okay, yeah, we eat them. That's a bummer, if you're a cow. But we've always eaten them, so why has it taken this long for them to get ticked off? Now if the price of grass was sky-rocketing the way milk has, then sure, I could understand a few angry Holsteins.

These thoughts came to mind the other day when I was buying a gallon of milk. I mean, seriously, four bucks a gallon? What's going on with that? A gallon of gas - which is made from the remains of extinct reptiles - costs half that. And unlike cows, dinosaurs have good reason to be ticked off. First of all, they're, uh, well, dead. And then, to add insult to injury, puny ape-like creatures are digging up their remains, refining it, and burning it off into the atmosphere to join cow exhaust. RIP, indeed. Meanwhile, cows chew their cud, contentedly farting away our ozone layer.

So I got on the Internet to try and figure out what was going on. Fighting my way through pop up ads I finally found the site I was looking for. Yep, ESPN. I browsed through the sports scores, scanned the batting averages, and just generally had a good time.

Afterward, I took out a loan to finance a glass of milk, and remembered my quest. Oops. Darned tangents. I just can't keep off them. But I'm a guy, so it's all right.

So I got back on the Internet, ignoring the siren song of ESPN, and found an announcement by the U.S. Department of Agriculture that our national dairy herd is shrinking! What with higher costs, including in the price of soybeans, which are used to make Purina Cow Chow, dairy farmers have sold or slaughtered much of their cows.

Cows are on the decline. On their way out. Going the way of the dinosaurs. No more cows on Old McDonald's farm. No more "Moo Moo, Here and Moo Moo There." Humans in millions of years will be digging up their fossils, wondering about the horned mammal with four stomachs responsible for turning the entire planet into a steamy rain forest. So I urge you to get out to the countryside now. See the Bessiesaurus before she's extinct.

Just don't get too close to the tail.

Man's Best Friend

I was doing the world a favor, showering the stink off after working outside. Meanwhile, the cat, whom I affectionately know as 'the cat,' was pacing outside of the shower, occasionally poking a paw through the shower curtain. He was meowing his feline head off.

"What's up, buddy?" I asked, not expecting any more of a response than I'd get from my teen-aged daughter. I wasn't disappointed. He just looked at me quizzically.

Mystified, I finished up my shower, thinking that I never know what he's thinking. That got me to wondering that my dog is definitely a better communicator than the cat.

I know when he's happy. I know when he wants out, when he thinks he's in trouble, when he wants to play, when he'd like the popcorn bowl to just magically slip out of my hands. I know his happy bark, his excited bark, his angry bark, his 'hey, are you a gopher?' bark.

And it's not a one-way street. He understands me, too. "Good dog!" "Bad dog!" "Hey, get out of there!" "You be good!" "Don't poop there!" "Stupid dog! Do you really have to mark **everywhere** you go?" He knows what these phrases mean.

I tested him once, just to see if he actually understands English. If I say excitedly, "Do you want to go for a walk?" he gets all excited. So one day, I said, "do you want to go for a walk" in a normal tone of voice. He cocked his head and looked puzzled. Then I said the same thing in Spanish, and, ...get this!... he gave me the **same** cock-headed puzzled look, ...this time in Spanish! Since a dog is like a guy (always pretending to be dumb), this proved that he understood me perfectly well.

Not the cat, though. He has exactly three thoughts that he bothers to communicate. One, "Hey, stupid human, feed me." Two, " Hey, stupid human, make room so I can sleep in your lap." And three, "Hey, stupid human, would you open the damned door, so I can chase that robin?"

He makes no attempt to understand me, though. If I try talking to him, he just gives me a superior look, and pads off somewhere to find a sunbeam to stretch out in.

So does this signify intelligence?

My wife thinks so. She figures that the less you talk, the more intelligent you are. As Abraham Lincoln said, "It is better to remain silent and be thought a fool, than to open ones mouth and remove all doubt." The bible agrees, by saying "The words of the wise are few and even a fool is thought to be wise when he holds his tongue" - Proverbs 17:27,28

I don't see good news for me here. Because, in my family, this ranks me intellectually somewhere between the parakeet and the dog.

Pet store Wisdom

I remember reading somewhere that you can't catch anything from your dog, like a cold or flu, nor can he catch yours. Nothing is really communicable between humans and their pets, unless you have a pet monkey or a little boy or something. While I don't have any scientific proof yet, I suspect this is a falsehood.

The thing that got me wondering about this, and which enabled me to pierce the veil of secrecy perpetuated by the lobby for Purina Puppy Chow, was a disclaimer I had to sign when we purchased a parakeet for my daughter.

But first, allow me to digress for a moment. Did you know that Americans purchased more food for our pets last year than we spent on baby food? I believe this because Tender Vittles tastes **way** better than Gerber Strained Beets; and because I heard the same sucking sound coming from my wallet at the pet store that I heard when I took the kids to ChuckE Cheese to spend huge dollars on plastic bits worth pennies.

Sam's new parakeet, Ricky, cost $9.95. Not so bad, huh? Plus an extra dollar for an 'exotic' parakeet (which simply means it costs more for a different color nature determined not best for survival in the wild).

But by the time we left, we spent another $35 for a cage, $3.29 for food, $3.59 for sand grit, $2.39 for a calcium bone, $1.59 each for two perches, $2.89 for birdie treats, $1.89 for poop paper, $19 for birdie Jacuzzi, $1.15 for birdie beak brush, $59 for birdie toilet paper, $9.99 for a year's subscription to *Birds of a Feather*, and a little birdie computer complete with a one year subscription to AOL.

Then, the salesman, hoping I'd be stunned out of suspicion, whipped out an affidavit bigger than my ego, with legal mumbo jumbo in a font so small that would take an electron microscope to make out, and told me I had to sign it. He said it was an indemnity to release the pet store from legal responsibility should we catch a communicable disease which humans can catch from parakeets. With a smarmy car salesman smile, he assured me that the risks were absolutely minimal, and he could scarcely believe I had to sign the paper, but still watched carefully to be sure I signed away their legal responsibility.

As I drove away, the back of the car swaying from the load of bird stuff, I mulled over this communicable thing. My dog gets a distemper shot, yet, doesn't he provoke mine whenever he pees on my deck instead of venturing out into the rain? And what about rabies? Can't we get rabies from animals? Rabies became such a big issue that even the lobby for Purina Puppy Chow had to admit to its existence.

I started trembling. We **are** in danger of catching our pets' diseases!

We got home, and I slumped shakily into my chair. Then Buster strolled into the room, stretched, and took a calculated look at me. Then, with an insidious grin on his canine face, as if he knew what I was thinking, deliberately and provocatively ….. yawned.

I shuddered, and tried manfully to stifle the urge, as, all of a sudden, I, …I… yawned, too!

Mosquitos

Marv Albert got what was coming to him. Remember him? The sports announcer who jumped on a woman's back in their hotel room and bit her while wearing a toupee, white panties and garter. Thank God our justice system stood behind women by protecting them against ugly men who wear women's clothing.

But unfortunately, the justice system can't repair the irreparable damage my imagination took when it, upon hearing the details of his assault, tried to construct a visual for my brain. I tried to stop it, but I couldn't.

As I read the sordid details in the paper, I glanced at the picture of Marv that accompanied the story, and my mind, **totally without my permission**, drew this really detailed picture of him standing on a hotel bed, wearing white Victoria Secret panties and garter **not** meant to adorn a middle-aged man's hairy, lumpy legs!

As I mentioned, we did the right thing, proving we can and will protect women in our society. I have two girls, and I don't think you can do enough to protect the fair sex from the brute sex. Women don't have the natural protection afforded to say, the black widow, who controls when, how, and finishes by biting something off.

But there's another lady insect out there, who has no such protection, and of whom human law actually condones immediate execution upon sight. This insect is, of course, the mosquito. But we are doing the wrong thing. The only reason the female mosquito bites (it is only the female that bites) is because she ran into a big bulked-up male mosquito that was on steroids and a major league baseball contract. Have you ever seen a male mosquito? He's about ten times the size of the female, and looks like a flying daddy long-legs.

God didn't provide the female mosquito with a natural lubricant, KY jelly or Quaker State Super Blend SAE 10W-30 oil; so, in order to lay her eggs, she finds an unwilling blood donor, injects a sterilizing, numbing solution under the skin, and draws out what she needs.

If it wasn't for the fact that this solution causes an allergic reaction in the donor (well, plus a few nasty life-threatening diseases, too), he wouldn't even notice the minuscule amount she drew out. This blood, the lubricant, is used to ease the eggs out of her body during the egg-laying phase.

Why was all of this necessary? Well, it was because this big, brutish male jumped her and bit her back while wearing a toupee.

Have you ever swatted a male mosquito? Of course not, you probably never realized what one looked like. Meanwhile, you're punishing the poor female victims of a male assault. We ought to be out there smacking at the guy. Don't take it out on the lady.

She's only trying to alleviate pain, and perhaps death from a lubrication-less hatching.

I thought about this the other day when a big male mosquito floated in a sauntering way into our house. He flew around, all macho and pumped from his conquests, feeling invulnerable to punishment because society always blames the female.

"Society won't hurt me," he thought, buzzing around in his little toupee, white panties and garter.

"Nonsense," I said, as I squished him with my thumb.

The Wonderful Weasel

I think it's time we cut the little weasel a break.

Ha Ha Ha Ha Ha. .... I'm not talking about the President, either. Silly you.

I mean the furry creature, the real weasel. The oft-maligned egg stealing rodent.

And that's just the first misunderstanding. The weasel isn't really a rodent, it's an attorney. Just kidding, I mean, carnivore. The attorney is a rodent. And, um,... most Presidents are attorneys. So, that makes... uh, well, okay... Where was I going with this?

Anyway, the weasel gets too much bad press. How many times have you heard the phrases, "you lying little weasel!" or "don't try to weasel out of it" or "you have a weasel in your shorts"?

Do these bring up positive connotations?

And what is it with that "Pop Goes the Weasel song?" Are we talking about a bubble-gum chewing weasel? I think not.

The weasel deserves a lot more respect, like its cousins the raccoon, badger, wolverine and mink. It is a wily hunter, fearless, agile, with commando-like stealth abilities. They are as aggressive as a wolverine, as relentless as a woman shopper the day after Thanksgiving. And they're smart, too. Have you ever seen a dead weasel road kill? Thought not. They're way too smart to wrestle with a Toyota.

Most of the weasel's bad rap is due to its tendency to steal eggs. If so, it's not fair. Give them a break. It's not like they can purchase eggs at the local supermarket. They aren't preferred credit risks for Visa or Mastercard, because as a species they have a habit of running up their charge card bills and ruining their credit. Courageous, yes. Wily, yes. Thrifty, nope. They just gotta have that big screen TV.

Not only that, I think it's time that some college football team named itself The Weasels. After all Michigan has the Wolverines and Wisconsin has the Badgers. So how about changing the Washington Huskies to the Washington Weasels? Kinda has a ring to it, huh? Makes more sense, too. Huskies are in Alaska, not Washington. You ever seen a dog sled mushing around the Lincoln Memorial? I mean, really, give me a break. (Oh, Washington State? Sorry)

Wisconsin would have taken the name, but apparently the Weasel Union won't allow it. There's some kind of backlash for a heinous joint study at the University of Wisconsin and Michigan State University. Seems these schools, who.. get this.. pride themselves on academics, are in reality brain thieves!!!

Do you hear me!!! Brain thieves!!!

If you're a mammal, don't go anywhere near either of these universities. They are hoarding brains, including human brains(!!!), and posting pictures in something they laughingly refer to as their "Comparative Mammalian Brain Collection."

You don't believe me?? Okay, check it out yourself at www.brainmuseum.org. Then email your apology to me.

In fact, maybe you ought to get out there and visit them yourself. And while you're there, check out their rare collection of President's brains. Just don't blink when you go by that section. You might miss it.

And, most of all, don't ever turn your back on any "scientists."

Left-Wing Politics

Someday I'm going to get serious, and try to understand politics. I feel if I put a concerted effort into this study, I will understand the difference between a liberal Republican, and a conservative Democrat.

I also think there should be more avian ways to describe people's martial tendencies. You have your hawks, who want to go to war right now. You have your doves who want peace at all costs. So what would you call someone who wants to fight as a last option? Or someone who wants a preemptive limited precision strike with immediate mediation? Or someone who wants peace, but only if they get their way? Or how about someone who simply wants to argue all the time?

I think the seagull is the perfect symbol for this last person. Have you ever seen seagulls fighting amongst themselves? I was eating lunch at a Park District once, where a lot of gulls hang out waiting for some handouts. I noticed one gull, who was defending a five foot radius next to my window. If I were to throw out a piece of my lunch, it was his. And if any other gull came near, this gull would squawk and chase it away.

And why do gulls have different-colored feet? Is it an age thing, or are they different types of gulls? They looked like the same breed to me, but some had yellow feet, some were orange, and some were some kind of gray.

I think the answer is that their feet colors indicate their political leanings, such as yellow for 'left wing', orange for 'right wing' and gray for moderate.

On a purely offhand note, did you know you can spell grey as either gray or grey?

The goose

I'd pay money to see it, I thought to myself, looking through the glass at the goose. And I wouldn't get mad about it, either.

The goose in question was standing next to the office door, between my car and me. He was nibbling at a cigarette butt, probably trying to figure out why we stupid humans take a perfectly good leaf, wrap it in paper, put fire on one end and suck on the other end. Put that way, it's a pretty good question, even for a bird-brain.

Anyway, what I would pay money for would be to see this big guy do a flip. Or even a cartwheel. That'd be okay, too.

I'm sure most of you are following me, but the rest of you, I'll give you some background.

The Canada goose and his wife have taken up residence under a sign, just twenty feet away from a busy highway. The nearest body of water is a dried out drainage ditch, and thousands of cars and trucks rumble past every day. But Mrs. Goose doesn't seem to mind the hustle and bustle, and went ahead and laid two eggs in the dirt at the base of the sign. They take turns sitting on the eggs and pooping out huge goose speed bumps in our parking lot.

I tried to imagine how they ended up here, and could only come up with two different scenarios. The first has them flying back up to Wisconsin from their winter home in Tennessee, and while banking through a turn, Mrs. Goose squawks, and honks, "Oh, no, my water broke." So, Mr. Goose glides down with her to the nearest patch of green, where she does Lamaze before finally laying her eggs.

Or, in my opinion, more likely, Mrs. Goose, tired of life in the country, with marsh grass, bugs and cow manure, convinced her husband to move her to a condo in the big city, close to Starbucks.

So while I waited for Mr. Goose to mosey away, I wondered what it is about acrobatic birds that cause road rage. Sure, I wasn't happy that he was keeping me from my car, but I wasn't about to pull a gun and shoot anything. But there are a lot of people out there, especially the 'alleged' people who drive Grand Prix's, who wouldn't hesitate to run over granny if a bird was flipped at them.

Not me though. If I saw a bird flip, I'd just have to stop and applause. Think about it. Birds just aren't equipped for that kind of physical feat. Sure, wings help, but still it'd be a difficult maneuver. So if a bird flipped at me, I'd just have to stop and give it some money or some Canada Goose Kibbles & Bits or something. Make it feel appreciated.

So I'm going to watch and wait for the chicks to hatch. Then, when they leave their nest and waddle off towards the nearby highway, maybe they'll put on a show worth watching. Road rage indeed.

Seagulls

Sandy and I were relaxing on the deck, our eyes closed. A breeze (it was invisible, but we believed in its existence), warmed by the spring sun, tickled our bodies with a feathery touch. In the distance, seagulls raucously croaked their unlovely ballads.

The beach, right?

A marina or something?

Nope. Our backyards deck.

Fifty miles away from Lake Michigan. Nowhere near any substantial body of water. The closest water source are a few retention ponds and the Illinois River, still two hundred miles away from where it feeds into the Mississippi.

So what are seagulls doing here? We could do nothing about wonder.

A few days later, I was driving, a few miles from home, and my attention was drawn to a tractor turning over the field.

What drew my attention, you ask? The sound of the tractor's engine? The smell of freshly turned earth? The movement of the tractor?

None of these.

It was all of the white shapes, hovering and darting around the tractor. Digging in the upturned earth behind it. A huge flock of seagulls were diving and buzzing the tractor, cawing like mutant albino crows.

They were digging into the ground behind the tractor. I couldn't see what they were doing, but it was obvious that they were feasting on critters turned up by the farmer's plows.

So what would a plow turn up? There's only one answer, right?

Worms.

What the heck are seagulls doing trespassing on the domain of the most well-known worm hunter out there? The lovely robin?

Then it occurred to me. I'd recently seen seagulls encroaching on the property of another bird, the pigeon. I remembered once we were coming out of a pizza restaurant, where it shared a parking lot with a White Castle restaurant.

And there, in the middle of the parking lot, was a huge flock of seagulls, singing a really bad 1970's song to a synthetic piano. No, wait, wrong story. This flock was picking through the dumpster behind the White Castle, looking for artery-hardening snacks.

Are seagulls waging a hostile takeover of other birds' rights?

What next, are we going to see them fighting with Chickadees over bird feeders? Cramming their big white and gray butts in cages and trying to chirp? Sitting up in trees in the middle of the night, shouting "What?," er, "Who?" Painting their beaks colorfully, and appearing on cereal boxes to sell refined sugar disguised as food?

What can the other birds do to protect themselves?

Well, I suggest that they just turn it around and counterattack.

Yeah, get right back in their faces, and take their land.

I remember once reading about a company that started a hostile takeover of a competitor by aggressively purchasing its stock. The other company, totally opposed to being taken over, responded by turning around and buying up the first company's stock.

This frenzy went on for a few highly publicized weeks, each of them, in essence, eating each other, until third company got sick of it, and bought them both.

So next time you're at the beach, flipping frisbees at each other, don't be surprised if a flock of robins start wheeling overhead, diving at fish and chips.

More Birds

Why do coal miners take canaries down with them to help them detect when poisonous gases are present? As we all know, the canaries are meant to be an early warning system for the miners. If the birds start making little gasping noises, the miners start sprinting for the fire escape. I realize all of this, but why canaries? Canaries are cute, companionable birds that don't deserve this kind of fate. They should use some kind of bird we really don't care about, like vultures, grackles or Congressmen (I'm kidding about Congressmen. We all know they can't die of gas or they would have by now.)

But canaries? They aren't loud, or anything. There are plenty of loud, obnoxious birds out there that are fully capable of squawking a louder alarm than canaries ever could. The only thing I can think of is canaries are just the loudest chokers (outside the New York Knicks).

I wonder if seagulls are going to want this job, too?

...

Have you ever been pooped on by a bird? You know, one night you just feel a wet 'splort' on your head, and when your inquiring hand brings the offending article down for your face's inspection, you see a white, melted-marshmallow-type goob covering a little, black, hard excrement.

Well, of course you have. Everyone's been pooped on by a bird at sometime in his or her life. Kinda makes you wonder, though, have you ever been peed on by a bird? How would you know? One night a drop of moisture 'splinks' on your head. You probably look up and tell your companion, "Looks like it's going to rain."

Even on a clear evening that's the only thing your brain will allow you to think, especially since at night you're probably talking about **bat** pee.

Mayflies, which come out in May, as opposed to June bugs, who come out in June, lay eggs near ponds and streams. Its larvae is born in the water and lives for up to three years as an aquatic insect, eating underwater plants and small aquatic animals.

At a certain stage, they climb to the surface and molt, sprouting lacy, delicate wings.

And get this, they don't have mouths!

Because they have no mouths, they can't eat. They only live for a few hours or days, long enough to mate (using sophisticated hand signals, since the line "So, what's your sign?" is impossible to say without a mouth.)

After mating, they go back to the water, lay eggs, and die in masses (and I don't mean church).

Imagine what a better world it would be if we could splice the 'no mouth' gene into the genes of lawyers and telemarketers.

Chapter 9   Guys and driving off the range

Drivers

I was watching the comedian Gallagher once, and he did a little bit on bad drivers. He thought the best way to avoid bad drivers would be if all people were given big dart guns. Then, if you saw someone being an idiot, you simply shoot a dart at the car. That way, any time you see a car careening towards you with darts sticking out all over, you run for cover! It also makes it easy for the police to know whom to pull over.

I also thought it would be helpful to have personal message boards on the front and back of your car. You would have a keyboard in the car, and type little messages and love notes for drivers around you. Then I considered that I'd probably get into an accident as I'm looking to find the 'F' key while driving, and decided Gallagher's idea is better.

What was I going to type with the 'F' key? It's not what you think. I was going to type, "What a Fine Day!"

You believe me, don't you?

Beemer Envy

All right. I admit it. I have a bad case of 'Beemer Envy.'

You know, that angry feeling you emote towards every BMW, Lexus or Mercedes that effortlessly purrs past your little Beemer-wannabe Toyota or Saturn. The feeling is exacerbated by the fact that the typical driver of one of of these luxury cars feel that he's too important to wait his turn at merges or other traffic slowdowns; and zooms self-importantly past you on the shoulder, just so he can gain three seconds to go waste at the golf course.

If he was really so important, I'm sure that everyone at his destination would be more than happy to await his arrival, unless, of course, he's bringing the breakfast rolls or bagels.

So, while normally I enjoy opportunities to help other drivers enter a busy street, or let a semi-truck, who's blinking his turn signal, to enter or merge into my lane; perversely, I get a delicious thrill anytime I can thwart Mr. Beemer or Mr. Lexus. I just won't let them in. They just have to find someone else to butt in on.

One day, I was a witness to a driving miracle. Something you just don't see on a normal basis.

I was tooling down the Dan Ryan Expressway following a semi in the right lane. I pulled into the middle lane to pass, and saw what I couldn't see from behind the semi.

A full dump truck! And it was right in front of me!

One of my arms, reacting to a reflex considered long dormant, sprung up to shield my face from the inevitable spray of granite and debris that spews behind all dump trucks. Visions of sugar plums, er, cracked windshields leaped to my mind, and I quickly pumped the brakes, so some of the stones and concrete might actually miss my hood.

And then I noticed something. There were no projectiles zinging at me from the truck. Rocks weren't gleefully pinging against my car and ricocheting against the three other cars who were now close on my butt. We were in Chicago, after all.

I peered closely at the dump truck, and I saw something I never saw before or after on a dump truck. His load was, really, and I mean it,

Don' t be shocked

Only read this if you're around someone who knows CPR

His...load ....was ....tied down!!

(You know, I really don't mind debris-spewing dump trucks when I see them being tail-gated by Mr. Lexus or Mr. Beemer.)

Obnoxious Driver Awards

Have you ever been in traffic at a stoplight, listening to your favorite Dave Matthews tune, and some idiot pulls next to you, windows down, huge booming bass thumping mightily from speakers surely containing some kind of mutant woofers and tweeters?

You sit there, Matthews shouted down to a whisper, your car shaking like a vibrating bed from one of those cheap hotels. A cluttered thought tries to emerge from your bruised brain.

You try to capture the thought, a will-o-wisp, floating gently out of reach.

Finally, through the din, the thought coalesces, and you take hold of it,

and wonder....

....just wonder,

...if he really wants to hear the song better ....

Why doesn't he just put his damned windows up??!!!!!

On that note, we're going to have a little quiz today, and pick out the award winners for **The Most Obnoxious Drivers** awards.

Yayyyy!!!! (Clap, clap, clap!)

Now, if you recognize yourself in any of these, you live in a glass house. So what we (the rest of us) would like you to do, is to pick up a rock, ... take careful aim, ... and whack yourself between your own eyes!

(Smack!)

Yaaayyyyy!!!!

(This is the applause from considerate people who are forced to share the same roads with you).

However, I doubt if any bad drivers would read anything I'd write. They're all out there reading their tickets, juggling their court dates and driving with their knees.

So, without any further adieu, here are the award categories for **The Most Obnoxious Drivers:**

Category One: Those drivers who flick cigarette butts out the window, rather than use the ashtray that comes installed in most cars, including the Yugo!

Category Two: People who don't wave to acknowledge the courtesy of someone who lets them in, at the risk of really pissing off everybody behind, more than half of whom are armed.

Category Three: People who pull off a side street in front of you, ... while you're doing the speed limit (okay, five to ten miles over the limit.) ...., forcing you to slam on your brakes ... and there's nobody in sight behind you ...., so they could have waited two seconds.... then, half a mile later, force you to brake again when they turn off.

Category Four: People, or sub-humans with thick eyebrows who part their hairy backs down the middle, who wait until the last second to merge, passing as many people as they can, rather than taking their turn in line behind people who earned the right to go first.

Category Five: Someone who races you for the merge, sprinting up to twenty miles over the speed limit. And you let him, thinking to yourself, "Fine, at least he won't hold me up." And when he gets in front, he slows down to **under the speed limit!**

Category Six: All those people who will not let you in, when you are in a parking lot, and trying to pull onto a busy street, next to a light, where cars are slowing down anyway, so what's the big deal because it's not going to make them lose more than two seconds of their lousy worthless lives anyway.

Time to vote: (Please bear with us as we count the special, butterfly ballots we got for a discount from the State of Florida.)

Okay, voting's over.

I'll bet you're excited. You can't wait.

And, I'll bet you're wondering what the lucky winner is going to win. We'll tell you in a minute while we count all seven votes.

And the winner is....... Drum roll .... Drum roll continues .... Now the drum roll starts getting quieter as the drummer

realizes he will need to end the song ……… almost done
…….drum, drum, drum…….
Whoa,
We have a surprise winner. A write-in winner. Wow!
The winner of the Most Obnoxious Driver award is….
The Inappropriate Polite Guy!
You know this guy. As you're pulling up to a light that has just turned green, and you count your blessings that the timing is perfect and you'll get there just as traffic surges forward again. Then, the guy in front of you suddenly brakes to let some guy coming from the opposite direction turn left into the nearby White Hen Pantry.

Unfortunately, this guy, knowing he shouldn't be going, doesn't notice the guy in front of you holding up everybody, because he's trying to remember what he's supposed to get since his wife added a fourth item to the things he's supposed to pick up and he forgot to make a list, so he hesitates. Then your guy realizes his error, and lurches forward, just as the convenience store guy decides he'd better go.

So they both go at once, and slam on their brakes in alarm, and they do this once or twice more, as your underwear begins to twist and bunch.

Finally, the turning guy bursts through, just as the traffic light makes a serious mood swing from green to yellow.

Then the polite guy shoots through the yellow, and you're left sitting at red.

Which matches the color of your face.

(Oh, the winner receives a year's supply of road-killed skunks, whipped at their heads like frisbees by gas mask-wearing good drivers.)

Semi

I was on a cloverleaf getting ready to merge onto the highway. Peering over my shoulder, I looked onto the highway.

Just a hundred yards away, a big semi-tractor trailer rig was thundering at me through the atmospheric haze, leading a virtual stampede of roaring internal combustion metal hurtling towards me.

In fear, I slowed, thinking there was not going to be an easy merge for awhile.

Then, to my astonishment, the huge semi...

(I must digress here. Why is a huge tractor-trailer called a 'semi?' Just grab your Webster's dictionary, which defines semi as 'half, partly, not fully...' I think you'll agree with me that a semi, is not, in fact, semi-anything.)

Where did I leave off?

Oh, yeah,

...the huge semi, actually turned on its turn signal, and worked its way into the next lane, leaving a workable gap for me to squirt into.

As I pulled in, the semi passed me, and pulled into the space in front of me. I flashed my lights in appreciation for the kindness.

Then the shock hit. A considerate gesture, in Chicago, at rush hour!

Wow! I almost swerved into a ditch.

Then I noticed something on the back of the tractor trailer rig. There was an 800 number, and it said to call it with any comments.

So I dialed the number on my cell phone.

"Hello." A gruff voice answered, probably expecting yet another complaint. That's all people do, right? Complain?

"Hi," I said cheerfully. "I'm calling about truck number thirty-four."

"Yeah," the voice said warily. I'm sure my cheerfulness was throwing him. He was probably trying to recognize the unfamiliar tone, which usually only comes at him when he's ordering a Big Mac.

"I just want to tell you that truck number thirty-four is very polite and considerate," I said.

"Huh?"

"Yes. He let me merge into traffic, and was very helpful. I thought you guys should know this, and maybe give him a certificate of appreciation or something."

"Um, okay, we'll make a note of it," he said, his gruff voice croaking awkwardly into pleasant mode.

I hung up, feeling like maybe nothing was accomplished, but hoping something had been. Maybe someone would say something to the driver. Maybe the guy who answered the phone benefited from a dose of good will.

I've run across many semi drivers over the years, and I find that they are usually the most polite, helpful people on the roads.

But still, to do it in rush hour Chicago...

Do it sometime. If you see an eight hundred number on the back of a truck, go ahead and call it. Make someone's day.

Mergers

I remember coming up to a merge once, where the right lane was closed ahead. I pulled smoothly into the left lane, and am going the same speed as everyone else. We're moving towards the merge almost perfectly in line with each other, and it's comforting to realize that there won't be any jostling and jockeying for position. We're all respecting each other's place in line.

. Then some jerk behind me pulls out, and swings to the right with the obvious intention of passing as many people as he can before the merge. If he's lucky, maybe he can pass seven of us, and save as much as eight seconds from his commute. Like eight seconds of his life is worth anything.

Yeah ladies, it's always a man. Selfish bastards.

I think police should have the authority to use their nightsticks on lunkheads like this. A traffic ticket is worthless. These people in 75 mph bullets aren't stopped by a piece of paper.

What they really need is a good whack behind the knees, or maybe a couple hours in Canadian immigration.

And, I remember reading a bumper sticker once that said, "The only reason some people are alive is because it's against the law to kill them."

Oh yeah, and the sticker was on the bumper of a car passing a bunch of us before a merge.

...

Until Gallagher's idea of shooting darts at obnoxious drivers is passed (by a reluctant Senate), I'd like to pass along the following pointers for those responsible drivers (both of you) who don't want to be shot at:

- *Never use hand gestures, except polite applause for excellent rudeness.*
- *Never speed up to obviously block the path of an aggressive driver, time it to make it look like it was inadvertent.*
- *Never glare at someone who has performed driving idiocy. Look ahead and try to make it look like you having cut him off was innocent.*

Chapter 10 Guys and science

In Trivia Pursuit, guys take pride in being good at Science, while Arts and Entertainment freeze our brains. We also do pretty well at Geography, since there's no need to ask for directions.

Air

Pssst!

Wanna buy some air?

"Air?!" you say? "Why would I want to buy air?! Air is one of the most common substances on Earth. Heck, air is what makes Earth livable in the first place. We all use it, even animals and George Bush. It's continually renewed by plants and available every time you inhale. Why should I have to pay any money for it?"

Well, you already do.

In fact, you buy air all the time.

I thought about this the other day when I was buying bubblewrap to protect some stuff that I was going to ship. Being a guy, the first thing I did with the bubblewrap was to pop a bunch of the little bubbles. Wheee! Pop! Pop! Pop!

Uh-hem, sorry.

Anyway, then it occurred to me. I had just purchased air.

Think about it. Bubblewrap is basically just two ingredients: air and plastic. If not for the air, the little sheet of plastic would be worthless, since it wouldn't protect anything. So basically, the air is more important than the plastic.

Not so for potato chips. How many times have you bought a big, fat bag of chips, ripped it open, had a bunch of air whoosh past your face, and found yourself with a bag of crumbs?

Still, though, there are times when you buy the air, because you need air. Like you know it's time to buy new tennis balls when they go flat. And when your tires are low, you'll plug fifty cents into an air compressor with a faulty gauge and a leak in the hose, and the air hisses out everywhere but into your tire, while you mutter and cuss.

Or maybe if you're planning a space or underwater trip. In fact, it's a little known fact that NASA has been exploring the possibility of bringing bags of potato chips on future missions to furnish the astronauts with their air and food needs.

But it's not just air, either. You also buy water, ... and dirt ... and poop!

Poop, you say?

Yeah, poop. Can you say 'fertilizer'?

The most common substances on Earth. We buy them.

Not only that, but we're willing to spend extra money to get them from other places. We'll think nothing of spending two bucks for some Artesian water from France or the Fiji Islands. Heck, most people don't even know that 'artesian' simply means well water from water drained from higher ground. So we're spending extra money on well water?!

Sheesh.

Everybody knows that the best water comes from drinking fountains in high schools. Not the porcelain ones. The metal ones. The best water in the world, if you don't mind the slight Juicy Fruit flavor from a piece of gum some freshman wedged into the spout.

Anyway, I want in on this scam. I want to sell something that's a common source. Something renewable and everyday. Something you wouldn't normally think of buying. In fact, something I find every morning, in my drain.

Pssst!

Wanna buy some hair?

Soft Rocks

One year, we took a trip out to Iowa to visit Sandy's sister. After a nice relaxing swim in the pool, I went back to the room to shower. To my surprise, I was barely able to work up a lather with the soap, and my body felt really sticky. Thinking it was just cheap, hotel soap, I grabbed the nice, expensive shampoo that Sandy won't travel without, and started washing both of my hair. Again, I was barely able to soap my head ('soap', not 'soak').

After drying off, I relayed this phenomenon to Sandy, who wisely nodded her head, and with professor-type decorum (since she has devoted much time to everything related to hair-washing) informed me that the hotel has 'hard' water, whereas, we have 'soft' water at home.

As a retired lifeguard (meaning Speedos no longer look good on me), I couldn't remember ever hearing about any difference in water's 'hardness', and definitely don't remember any soft-landing belly-flops. So, I asked her what made our water at home softer. She replied saying that our water softener softens our water by adding salt.

Huh?

I thought to myself, "Self, how can this be?" Salt, I reflected, is a crystal, which I'm pretty sure is in the rock family. So I was being asked to believe that you **add rocks** to make water **softer**!

Uh, huh. And you gain weight if you want to fly, right?

I saw a documentary once that showed rock being blasted out of quarries, and taken by truck to processing plants that munched the rocks into a pasty-like substance that they spread out onto long roles of paper. Then they rolled more paper on top of the sludge, and cooked everything in a big oven. Cutting it up into sheets, they shipped the completed drywall to job sites to be nailed to studs (those good-looking, manly, macho 2X4's holding up your walls).

Where am I going with all this?

Um, oh, yeah.

Be patient. We're almost there.

The point is that since drywall is made from rock, you can't escape the fact that, after all these years, we still live in caves!

And I'm not done yet!

You can even take this thought a little further. Because, if you think about it, we even drive rocks!

Take your basic car. It's manufactured out of steel, which comes from iron ore, which is a **rock**! Even tires come from rubber, a plant that grows in rock.

So, what's that make us?

Let's review. We live in caves. We drive around in mobile rocks. We sometimes wear animal skins.

Somehow Fred Flintstone doesn't seem so primitive anymore.

(Oh, by the way, I'm going to make my snowballs this winter out of soft water, so I don't hurt anyone.)

...

If anyone knows the answer to this question, and has some kind of scientific proof (a letter from your Mom would be okay), please let me know:

If two people were going from point A to point B in a rainstorm, which one would get wetter, the one who sprints, or the one who walks? (I took a peek out the window a few minutes ago, and have a vested interest in the answer, since my umbrella is out in the car)

My own personal opinion, in case you're interested, is that they would get equally wet, except the person who runs will be wetter in the front, while the one who walks is just as wet, but with the wet spread more equally. Unless you skip, in which case the rain will, strangely enough, leave you alone. Most people will, too, especially if you're a guy.

Natty

There are a lot of compliments you can pay people, but always make sure the person you give them to thoroughly understands that you are paying them a compliment. There is a woman in our office, who always is so neat, prim and orderly, that I couldn't help one morning but to tell her, "Terri, you certainly look natty today." She arched her perfectly plucked eyebrows, and asked dangerously, "Natty?! What's that supposed to mean?" Clearly 'natty' looks and sounds too much like 'ratty;' and clearly 'natty' raised negative connotations in her mind.

Together, with me sweating copiously, nervously praying I'd remembered the definition correctly, we looked it up, and Webster bailed me out by defining natty as "...trim and smart in appearance or dress." A near-death experience indeed.

Another thing you can compliment people with, is calling them 'bumpy brain.' Science studies have shown that the deeper the crevasses in your brain, the better able you are to use it. That's why you smack someone on the head if they are being obtuse. You are trying to deepen the crevasse and make them smarter. I think this is why smart people (with deep crevasses) are called 'deep thinkers,' while the smoothies are 'shallow thinkers.' They are really referring to the depth of folds in the brain. So if you want to call somebody smart, just tell them they have a bumpy brain today.

If they're so smart, they'll figure it out.

Clouds

I was driving to work one day, and even though it was spring, there were 'fall' clouds out. If you really think about it, there are different clouds in the different seasons. During the winter, they are just big grey (or gray), ill-defined clouds, merging together into a murky dolphin-reminiscent gray. You can suffer through weeks without seeing the blue of the sky.

During the spring, you'll usually see big black and white rain clouds, which dump on you one minute, and then go scurrying off to answer a raindancer elsewhere. In the summer, two types emerge: one, scientifically named, 'The Big Cotton Candy' cloud, comes out to shade you every five minutes from overcooking, and to remind you to turn over. The "Wispy Leftover' cloud are just the bits of the 'Big Cotton Candy' cloud that fall off when the big guy runs off to escape the moon at dusk.

So that morning, when I was driving to work, I was looking at the angry, cold fall clouds that were so out of place that spring morning, and I started wondering how much a cloud weighs. I know, there are different sized clouds. But how much, per cubic whatever, do clouds tip the scales at? I'm guessing, that since they are probably quite hefty, with all that rain water and lightning in them, so what's to stop them from plummeting to the ground, to bounce off the earth and knock coffee onto the lap of a litigation-happy woman at McDonald's?

So I looked it up. Those beautiful fluffy clouds that float over your head, lighter than air, aren't lighter than air!! Do you know that a good sized nimbocumulous cloud weighs MILLIONS of tons, and soars up to 60 **thousand** feet above the ground??!!!!! And all of this weight is just hanging over your head.

Those suckers are stuffed with huge amounts of ice crystals and moisture condensation, and charged with raging electrons, ready to lash out at the earth to hit my neighbor, who I saw sitting under a tree in the last thunderstorm. Even one of those wispy cirrocirrus floating tantalizingly just 35,000 feet over your head, still weighs more than a Chrysler mini-van!

Ever since I thought of that, it's started taking me longer to get places. After all, it's pretty hard to get around when you're avoiding driving under clouds.

...

Maybe clouds do fall from the sky. I think that's what fog is! Fog is just a cloud that gained too much weight and fell to the earth. So I start wondering if maybe we can get rid of dangerous fog by helping clouds keep the weight off (I think clouds already try doing this by hanging around water, where they should weigh less, but they have the same mass).

Anyway, if we could figure a way to do this, we could clear up a lot of foggy places like London and George Bush's head. As you know, Londoners drink too much hot tea, and all of the steam goes up into their atmosphere, with the result that their clouds overeat, causing them to rapidly gain weight and finally fall to earth to screw up their traffic. The answer is clear, we have to send Richard Simmons to England!

This solves two dilemmas, London can become a beautiful, sunny vacation spot; and we get rid of Richard Simmons for a while.

Physics

Last year, in my once a year golf outing that I do several times a year, I was standing behind a big oak tree, mulling over how best to maneuver my ball back onto the fairway. I was wondering whether to punch it under with a three-iron, or use up a couple shots and go around.

My friend Glenn, patiently (because his beer was still full and cold) waiting for me in the golf cart, said, "Trees are eighty percent air. You could probably just hit it towards the branches and have an eighty percent chance of it going through."

The logic seemed sound, but three shots later Glenn was cowering behind another tree from ricochets. I decided to go around.

Trees seem to violate rules of physics. Take a look at one. Think about it. It's top heavy. Try balancing some blocks like a tree. You can't do it. There's only one trunk, skinny in relation to the rest of the tree, and it supports bark, leaves, widely spreading branches, owls, monkeys, and the wish-it-was-rare yellow-bellied telemarketer. The amount of weight just from the leaves is staggering (as I re-discover every fall).

And I have to wonder how much weight a tree gains every time it rains. A good-sized maple probably doubles the load it carries. Added to this is the tremendous pressure exerted by wind on a blustery day.

But I don't want anyone to explain why trees don't tip over. I don't want to hear how that tree's roots counterbalance the branches, with the trunk providing a fulcrum point with E=MC squared, plus the divider of the radius being 3.1415, and do trees make a sound when they fall in the forest and no one is there to hear it, and ... etc. etc. I just want to add it to the list of miracles God quietly performs for us every day.

...

I don't know about you, but if I were dropped on a deserted island, I would lead a Gilligan-type existence as opposed to a Professor-type existence. I use computers, telephones, microwave machines, bananas and other modern tools every day; but stick me on a deserted island, even with all the raw ingredients necessary, and I couldn't make a spoon.

Look inside your radio. Do you even faintly understand transistors? We aren't children of technology, we just borrow it.

Ponderables
I just want to answer a few questions that have puzzled scholars and gentlemen in all the lands:

1) *When a tree falls in the woods, and there is no one to hear it, does it make a noise?* No, it doesn't. Everybody knows trees don't talk. And even if they did, they wouldn't cry out for help if they knew no one was there to catch them. And, in the remote chance that Tarzan was swinging by, there's no way he would be able to catch the tree anyway. And, of course, as we all know, noise is simply a wave vibration that travels aimlessly until it discovers some ugly fold of skin on the side of someone's head, where it will proceed to beat on some

kind of bongo drum that this person's brain translates into a kind of crashing sound.

2)   *When you install toilet paper, should the paper hang next to the wall, or away from the wall where it can be easily grasped, rather than trying to pry a fingernail under the paper as it adheres to the wall like caulk on a computer?* I think Ann Landers spent entirely too much time on this question, which answers itself. It's just a variation on the PMS-moon-women- slogan, "Put the toilet seat down!" This is what we get for inventing indoor plumbing. Almost every guy I know is perfectly comfortable in a portable john or weeing on a tree. But women wanted privacy, then they wanted a place to sit, then they want to be indoors, now the toilet seat has to be down, and finally, should the paper hang next to the wall or away from the wall? I rant, let's move on.

3)   *Should the toilet seat be left down or up?* Who cares?!

My wall is amazing. When I took that physics class in college, which you can see definitely (along with Gallagher) helped shape my life, I learned another interesting tidbit that I will share with you since my wife isn't interested. For every action, there is an equal and opposite reaction.

The example my prof' used to illustrate this was to say that if you push on a wall, it pushes back with the exact same force that you are exerting on it.

I tried his on my wall the other day, and sure enough, when I leaned on the wall, it didn't budge! Ever more, when I suddenly let go, my wall was so talented, it let stopped pushing **at the exact same time**! It didn't stumble or anything. I tried it a bunch of times, trying to trick it, but couldn't fool it once.

Philtrum

Two of the stranger mysteries God hasn't unveiled yet are,

1. *Why are newborn babies' first poops so hard to clean?*
2. *What is our philtrum for?*

If you ever had a new baby (you'll look really harried), the nurse will wheel up with a cart with baby supplies, including diapers, wipes and assorted powers, and encourage you to get acquainted with your new bundle of chubs.

The true reason they do this is because they don't want to be the person who has to clean up baby's first poops, which are a sticky tar-like substance best suited for gluing the reentry tiles on the space shuttle. This black gunk will not come off short of using turpentine or paint remover, both of which are not allowed in the hospital for fears of setting off some of the oxygen tanks and blowing up the hospital.

Actually, a well-placed charge of dynamite just might be enough to blow this stuff off your baby's gluteus.

The other question relates to the best-known part of your body, the philtrum. As you undoubtedly know, this is the vertical indentation between your nose and upper lip. This little groove's only known purpose is to provide a streambed for snot to go from your kid's nose to lip, only to get licked off (a deliberate action meant to gross out every adult in sight).

In adulthood, the philtrum serves no purpose, other than providing a part for a man's (and some unfortunate women) moustache.

...

More questions I would some day like to know the answer to:

Why are yawns contagious? How do scientists know no two snowflakes are exactly alike? How come I can remember my childhood address and phone number, but can't remember if today is Tuesday or Wednesday. If our bodies are 85% liquid, how come we don't leak?

Mass Diet

Let's go back to the subject of women and gravity. If you really think about it, women don't try to lose weight. They are actually trying to lesson the force of gravity between them and the bathroom scales. If our gravity were to suddenly lessen to, say, point nine Gee's, every woman in the world would lose 10% of her weight. However, she would still look the same. Would she be happy with her newfound weight loss? I don't think so.

So the proper thing to do now is for everyone to realize that women don't really want to lose weight, hence gravity. They want to lose mass! So starting today, women, you want to go on a mass-reducing diet. "So Kathy, you look great, how much mass have you lost?"

I know the above statement seems chauvinistic, at least it does to me. It's well known that many men are overweight, and are very interested in dropping a few pounds. Dropping pounds is in no way limited to women.

But men can drop weight much more rapidly than women. All we have to do is shake our heads, and let some of the rocks dribble out.

Also, do you know that a fish is mostly just a big muscle? Just think, a fish can move in water faster than we can move unassisted in air, which is far less dense. That's because they are propelling themselves, with sideways motion no less, by one huge muscle making up more than 60% of their bodies.

Density is a very interesting property. You can go from solids to liquid solids, like mercury, to liquids and gasses. And if you really think about it, solids are not solids. There are spaces between every molecule of solid, so basically solids are not, in fact, solid.

Where was I leading with this?

Oh yeah, if you could change our atmosphere to something lighter, like helium, women might just obtain that weight loss they were looking for.

No wait, that would result in weight gain.

You would need to weigh someone in a denser medium, like water, to make him weigh less. So maybe the answer is to melt the polar icecaps. Maybe women would be so happy about their weight loss, they wouldn't mind PMS, and we could keep the moon. No, that wouldn't work either, because if we were surrounded by water, we'd go under when the tide shifts.

Chapter 11   Guys and word play

Guys are like otters. We like to play games. It doesn't always have to involve a ball.

K/Cathy

I have a little game I play when I meet someone named (K/C)athy. I try to guess whether her name starts with a K or a C.

I think whoever decided to simply start spelling names differently, just for the sake of originality should be locked up with someone else's three-year old, Kool-aid stained, gummy-bear-slimed, bug torturing, over-Y-chromosomed, puppy-tailed boy!

Who cares if it's Shawn, Shawon or Sean; or Alison, Allyson or Allison; or Glen, Glenn or Glennnn; or Aritha or ...um...?

Anyway, if they really want to be original, just make up a name! Don't just spell a like-sounding name **differently**! AAAARRRRGGGGG!!!! I knew somebody who was, really, named Glen Glenn, and someone else named Robert Robertson.

For Crying Out Loud!

The people who do something like this have proven, beyond the eclipse of a doubt, that they are descended from the same idiots who helped create the goofiest language in the world.

Where else would you have words like bark (as in on a tree) or bark (what the animal says who pees on a tree); or 'to', 'too', and 'two'? These are three different words made by uttering the same sound. I read somewhere that the Eskimos have over one hundred words just for snow! And we can't even give the second integer its own sound! Try explaining this to your children! (pant, pant.... pause for a deep breath)

Okay, maybe there's a fix for all this stuff.

Like, let's try substituting the Spanish 'dos' for two: so you would count, "one, dos, three, four..." – but wait!

We can't have our fourth integer sounding like 'fore' and 'for'. Let's substitute the Japanese 'chee' (this is how it sounds, I'm not sure how to spell it). Okay, let's try again ... "one, dos, three, chee, five, etc."

That's better, but what do we do about those silent letters that someone stuck into certain words just to be obnoxious? If the 'k' in knee doesn't have anything to say, then get it out of there!!

I have to stop talking about this, because my ! key is getting kind of hot.

Myself

Guess what time it is? Time to vent again! Yaaaayyy!!!!! Wheeeee!!!!

And can you guess what it's going to be about this time?

I thought not.

Even I, myself, am not too sure.

Ha! I lied. But the sentence above should have given you a hint. And I'm sure those of you with bumpy brains not only figured what it meant, but also figured out what I was going to say. Which is pretty darned good, considering I don't know, myself.

Look! There was another hint! Did you get it this time?

Okay, okay, I'll get to the point.

Michael Jordan, you know him? Bald guy? Bad knees?

Anyway, Michael Jordan was interviewed once, and he said something along the lines of, "The other guys and myself really beat the pants off of Detroit."

Now do you get it?

That's right, the word 'myself.' The most abused word in the English language besides 'excuse me.'

Yeah, I know, 'excuse me' are two words. And they're abused for opposite reasons. "Excuse me" should be said more often, and 'myself' should be used less often.

Back to Jordan. And we don't mean that place out by Syria. What His Airness should have said is, "The other guys and I really beat the pants off of Detroit." Not myself.

Way too many people are using the word 'myself' instead of 'I.' And worse, it's people who should know better. Radio personalities, government officials, even teachers! These people should know better!

Not only that, but because they are getting radio and television time, their mistakes are being broadcast to a large audience, who all think to themselves, "Hmmm, Michael said, 'the other guys and myself.' He's a Floydillionaire, and a graduate of the University of North Carolina. He must be using the word correctly."

Then, at work, they all say, "The rest of the staff and myself are going out for lunch." And head off to go buy Mc-Whoppers.

I realize that this is way better than saying, "Me and the rest of the staff are going out for lunch." Of course, these are both wrong, even if you switch the 'me' or the 'myself' with 'the rest of the staff.' Either way you put it, it has to be 'eye.' Er, 'I.'

Aaaarggghhhh. It drives myself crazy!

The Letter 'C'

Now that I fixed the letter 'k,' it occurs to me that there's no need for the letter 'c' anymore. By fixing 'k,' we removed 'c's responsibility for the 'ka' sound, leaving 'c' with just the 'sa' sound, which is already capably hissed by the letter 's.' The solution is to simply drop the letter 'c' from the alphabet, right?.

This knocks (noks) the alphabet down to a more manageable and compact twenty-five letters. True, it plays havoc with 'The A,B,C Song,' but maybe a little creative rewriting would fix the part of the song where you have to rush the letters 'L,M,N,O,P,' which most kids merge into, 'Elm,N,Ah,Pee.' We'll also have to rename it, "The A,B,D Song.'

Someone else will have to volunteer to rewrite this, though, since I'm not a very good songwriter.

...

Now we're going to have to loan me to Spain to help them with their alphabet. Ever since I fixed the English alphabet, there's been call for me to address all of the extra letters in the Spanish alphabet. Most English-speaking people don't realize that the Spanish alphabet is longer than the English, especially since we dropped the letter 'c.'

The following characters are actually single letters in the Spanish alphabet, *ch, ll, rr* and *ñ.* The Spanish ran out of characters to make the 'cha' sound, the 'ya' sound, the 'dra dra dra' (rolling r's) sound, and 'nya' sound, so they just used double letters instead, and attached a leech to the 'n.'

While I'm not one to throw stones after our debacle with *to, too,* and *two,* I still think they were a little goofy. All they had to do was get some kind of artistic kind of dude to draw up a brand new character.

And if they needed up, they could have just contacted the artist formerly known as Pi, I mean, Prince.

More Alphabet Games

Hmmm, seems maybe I was wrong about the letter 'c.' It does, after all, serve a purpose, even if it has relinquished certain rights to the letter 'k.' The letter 'c,' besides being pleasing to the eye (although you are forced to loop counterclockwise against the right-handed grain, to make the character), does have a sound of its own other than the 'ka' sound and 'sss' sounds, which have been dibbsed by 'k' and 's.'

The letter 'c' is also responsible for making the 'cha' sound. Otherwise, you couldn't say words, like chair or chump or Charlie; or like birch or bitc..., or wrench or wench. I tried a few variations of other letters trying to make the same sound, but all I could manage at best was something like 'tsh.' I'm sure Charlie wouldn't like spelling his name, "Tsharlie." And 'T's don't like being this silent, anyway. You also couldn't change the name to Sharley, because it sounds too much like a girl, or an American deep-throated motorcycle. And we don't want to do anything like the Spanish did, where 'ch' is a single letter in their alphabet.

The only thing we can do is add the letter 'c' back into the alphabet. But we'll have to rename it, so it isn't pronounced 'sssseeee,' which is confusing because that's what our eyes (not I's) do.   We will use the Spanish pronunciation from now on, 'chay.' I know this messes up the 'ceee,' 'deee,' 'eeee' rhythm of the ABC Song, but that verse still needs work because of the whole 'L,M,N,O,P' part, anyway.

Any volunteers?

Alphabet

I want to get back to the letter 'k,' which is redundant or worthless, depending on when it's used. This letter has to be totally revamped.

As you'll recall, I vented earlier that if it's going to be silent, then get it out of there. Send it to the showers. Force it into retirement. Feed it to the telemarketers. Or, better yet, give it purpose.

I'm going to fix the whole nonsense right now. As of now, only 'K' will be used for the name Kcathy, and it will no longer be used for *knead, knife* and *Knewt Gingrich.* It will no longer be a cheap mimic of the hard version (R-rated) of 'C.' 'K' will henceforth represent only the 'ka' sound, with 'C' relinquishing its rights. *Cat* is renamed *kat,* and all *Cathy's* are now *Kathy's.*

The eloquent letter 'k' is restored!

Now only that, but this solution also fixes other problematic words, like *know.* We can keep the spelling, but simply pronounce it with the two syllables 'ka-no.' So when you understand something, you aren't telling people you don't. No longer will the phrase, "I know this," provoke the response, "What, you don't *no* this?" with you responding, "I said *know*, not *no!*"

Chapter 12   Guys and number

Of course, guys are good at numbers, be it golf scores, Fantasy League stats, baseball or girl's measurements.

Numbers

You get to witness another event here. I will, with proper reflection and consideration, name a number!

As you know, there is absolutely no limit to numbers. Pick the highest number you can think of, one hundred, fifty-gabillion, eight hundred-ninety five zazzquillion, three hundred-twelve, and you can get a higher number just by adding one to it. Or dos.

I must digress here, for to my dismay, I found that my new number for 'two' is faulty. 'Dos' is pronounced the same as dose, as in getting wet. It might also cause confusion in some of the Mafia circles where the common phrase, "Kill dos guys!" could cause Laurel and Hardy-type confusion.

"Kill dos guys, so we can gets dem to rat!" says the first hit man (meaning *those* guys, not *two* guys).

A second hit man replies, "Boss, ders chee (remember, this is the new number for four) guys dere. How many do I gotta rub out?"

The first one says, "Kill dos (meaning two) of dem and de others will squeal!"

127

The second hit man, starting to get a little cheesed, exclaims, "You sed dat, how many do I gotta erase?!"

The first guy is exasperated too, and angrily says, "Kill dem all! I don't care!" whereupon they never succeed in getting their prisoners to squeal.

We'll have to resolve this 'dos' issue later.

Anyway, the only thing that definitely cannot be finite is numbers (and the Universe, which is too scary to think about right now).

So today I decided to name a number, and immortalize it forever. The new number is, (are you ready?), ...

"Floyd".

Illions

What is an "illion"? Once you get beyond the comprehensible numbers like, one, chee, hundred, and thousand, you enter the "illion's". A billion, trillion, smillion, gazillion. Who dictated that there should be an "illion" with the higher numbers?

Until someone explains it to me, my new number, "Floyd" will remain "Floyd" without the accompanying 'illion.' If someone comes up with a reasonable explanation for the suffix 'illion,' I will gladly change my new number to "Floydillion." But, until they do, 'Floyd' will stay.

My kids wanted to get into the act and name their own numbers, too. Sam's new number was "dee dee." Lauren chimed in with the number "beautiful," and my wife Sandy chipped in with the number "wedgie," eyeing Sam mischievously.

Of course, the 'illion' rule remains in effect, and these may become "dee dee-illion," "beautifulillion" and "wedgieillion" if the proper proof of 'illion' be satisfactorily explained. Sam wasn't truly happy with just one number, and since there are infinite, also named the number, "ja-ka," or "ja-kaillion."

Floyd

The name 'Floyd' is kind of a joke around our household. Whenever someone is christening a pet or invisible friend, or naming any kind of thing, there has always been group discussion to find the best name. When we named our basset hound, many names were bantered around. One of the best names suggested was "Floyd," but I was resoundly voted down. I also suggested the name "Floyd" when the pet frogs were named, and the doll 'Baby Ka Ka,' and the toy giraffe 'Haack.'

The girls always giggled when I suggested 'Floyd' and they never consider the name. Sam thinks I made it up and jeers at me whenever I throw it in the hat.

The fact that they thought I made up this old-fashioned, but very real name, made me think of other names that are no longer used for new babies that weigh eight pounds, seven ounces, and measure nineteen inches, give or take head circumference.

And most of these old names already have faces associated with them. You know what Mable looks like, without me even describing her. Or Ethel, Fred, Art, Rose, Martha and Humphrey. They aren't young. Other names are on the cusp of becoming 'older people names,' such as Jennifer, Becky, Eric, Carol, Cindy and Ed. A few are making comebacks, though, like Sam and Alisa, with these names belonging to several generations. The popular names of today, and older generation names of tomorrow, are names like Lauren, Ashley, Tyler, Kyle and Andrea.

Personally, I think Floyd will make a comeback. Someday it will be more than just the barber on "Mayberry RFD"! It will return! And I will have helped!

Floyd, part dos

If you'll recall, earlier I discussed the need for a new name for the second integer to replace the word 'two,' which is *too* confusing *to* children, adults and telemarketers. I suggested we replace 'two' with 'dos,' which is the Spanish word for *'two.'* This worked fine until I was *dosed* with the realization that 'dos' is pronounced the same as 'dose,' as in to get wet. Unable to find a solution, I tabled the whole notion for later discussion.

After brainstorming for almost seventeen seconds, I'm ready to unveil my solution. As you know, I'm heading the campaign to bring the name 'Floyd' back into mainstream; and as part of my campaign I named the new number 'Floyd' (or Floyd-illion, depending on proof of the 'illion' rule), which is one of the higher valued numbers, falling in size somewhere between a gazillion and smillion.

Since my campaign is falling on deaf folds of skin filled with ear wax, I'm willing to withdraw my claim on the number 'Floyd' and allow it to be substituted for the second integer 'two.' I'm making this sacrifice, because I truly agree with all of you that there will not be a lot of need for my number with its current value higher than a gazillion; so I hereby release my claim for the betterment of our society. Reluctantly, I'm also dropping my campaign to bring the name Floyd back, too.

Please remember my sacrifice every time you hear your child counting, ..."one, Floyd, three, chee, five,..."

Perspective

I read once that the difference between a billion and a million can be put in perspective something like this: A million seconds is about eleven days. A billion seconds is more than thirty-one years!

Otherwise, doesn't sound like much of a difference, huh?

Okay, how about a trillion?

Can you say three thousand years!!!!!

Now do you really want to get scared?

Of course you do. You probably have all of the Alien episodes on DVD. You probably watch American Idol. You drive in bullets at sixty miles per hour, while other cars hurtle towards you at the same speed, missing each other by five yards. Heck, I can jump five yards.

So you asked for it. I'm going to scare you.....really good.

BWAH! Ha! Ha! Ha! Ha!

Here goes...

The national debt of the United States is Six.
Six what, you say?
Six,
not million,
not billion.
But Six **Trillion** Dollars!
That's over twenty-two thousand dollars for each and every single person in the United States. And every time another person is born, that person is automatically on the hook for twenty-two thousand clams. Welcome to reality. That, on top of the hospital charge, where you get to pay sixty bucks for an aspirin.

And that, my friends, is called perspective.

Perspective, Part Floyd

Speaking of perspective, it took one hundred and thirteen years to do it. And after all that time, it only lasted five months.
Do what?
Mary Dorothy Christian died in April 2003, at the age of 113 years and nine months.
The occasion that lasted five months?
Her tenure as the oldest person in the United States.
Imagine working at something for over one hundred and ten years, and then only getting to enjoy it for just a few short months.

The only thing I can compare this with is when my wife spends two hours making dinner, and then the kids take a perfunctory sniff, and turn up their little did-you-know-children-are-starving-in New Jersey noses at her hard earned efforts. Or when I wait in the doctor's office an hour for a seven-minute once-over.

Still though, think about it. You could live an entire 75-year average life span, and this lady still beats you out by almost four decades. Long enough for you to be born, grow up, have kids, and go to your kids' proms ... twice, and still have time to go out for an ice cream sundae. Split it in half and you could be a grandparent ... twice.

She was around for the eve of two different centuries, and lived in parts of three centuries (1800's, 1900's, 2000's).

One hundred thirteen years and nine months.

Are you staggered by this?

Do you need more?

Okay, the nine months alone is long enough to make an entire person from scratch. Yet, this is barely one half of one percent of her life span. In fact, you could manufacture 152 people, from conception to birth in the 1365 months of Christian's life. When she died, she was older than the cumulative ages of my wife, both kids, my daughter Lauren's pet rabbit and me.

She lived longer than the average life expectancy of a wolf, sheep, rat, horse, kangaroo, lion, monkey, mouse, parakeet, pig, rabbit, pigeon, common cold and hang nail all put together.

Even more remarkable, when she died, she was just **over** half the age of the United States of America!!!!

Not only that, but she did it with her favorite foods being Kentucky Fried Chicken and Hostess Twinkies

She took the crown in November 2002, following the death of Mary Parr, and passed the mantle along to Elana Slough, who takes control, also at 113 years of age.

I got on my handy dandy calculator, and figured how long before I might wrest the throne away. Hmmm just 69 years. That's only 36,266,400 minutes, or just 1.2 million episodes of M*A*S*H.

I can do it!

Pass me the Twinkies.

(P.S. do you think maybe the Department of Revenue could get $22,000 out of her estate, so we could handle her part of the national debt? Oh, they already do that? Well, okay, then.)

Baby Season

It's baby season at work again. I'm one of those weird people (big surprise, huh?), who, when I hear someone is expecting a baby, tries to calculate the day of conception. I think it is some kind of emotional attachment to Joseph, who I think definitely needs his own church (more on this later).

One of my fellow worker's significant other had a ten-pound, eight-ounce, twenty-two inch long baby. Another co-worker's sister had an eight pound, four ounce, nineteen-inch long baby. How do I know this? Well, they tell me. They're throwing out these vital statistics before they even tell what the sex is.

Why is it so important to know these things? Sandy made me memorize my kid's sizes, so that I could inform anyone who asked. When I saw baby pictures of myself, there they were, my weight and length, right on the back of the picture.

What the heck is this all about?

And this statistic, so important for a baby, becomes a closely guarded secret as people get older. I don't introduce myself to everybody like this, "Hi, I'm Norman Cowie, one hundred-seventy pounds, seventy-two inches." And I know women aren't going to introduce themselves this way.

The only thing I can figure out is that women want to know the size, so they can identify with the pain of birthing. That's why they 'oh' and 'ah' when they hear about ten-pounders. I disagree though, I think the most important statistic is the baby's head circumference. This more accurately illustrates the amount of pounding the birth canal absorbs.

Also, if I ever birthed an object more than five times the size of the exit, I doubt I would ever want to identify with anyone else's pain. After all, I am a guy. I would treat the news of the birth the same way I would look at an automobile wreck as I drive by.

I'd be hoping I don't see blood or pass out.

Baby Floyd

I had a baby once. I don't mean I really had a baby, but I learned from a reliable unnamed source (my sister-in-law K/Cathy) that I once suffered the same pain that most women (when not hooked up to an epidural, which is what 100% of men would insist on being hooked to if roles were reversed, assuming they would even consent to sex) suffer when they deliver seven-pound, three-ounce, nineteen-inch long babies into the world.

Once, when I was driving to a business meeting, I started experiencing waves of intense, searing pain in my abdomen. They would diminish for a couple minutes (I timed them) and then start again. I was sweating from the pain, which got so bad, I had to pull over and double over in pain. I was hurting so much that I stumbled out of the car and tumbled into the ditch next to the highway, curling into a fetal position on the ground, suit and all. I whimpered as waves of pain assaulted me.

I don't know how long I lay there, but I sure don't forgive the people who went whizzing by in my cars, probably barely casting me a curious glance (if I'd have had my Gallagher dart-gun, I'd have ….). After a while, the pain diminished enough for me to crawl back to my car and drive shakily home. I never went to doctors, which I think has helped me maintain my health, so I never officially learned what had hit me.

But Sandy said her sister K/Cathy had a spastic colon once, and compared its pain equally with that of childbirth. When I described my symptoms, she said they were very similar, so that's probably what it was.

I named my baby, 'Floyd.'

Time Travel
Time travel is possible, right now. Did 'ja know that? We have the ability, each of us, to change the rate of time without effort. This ability is instinctual and almost every one of us has traveled time, most without any clue they've done it.

Just today I traveled to the future, even as I typed the words you are reading right now. Spooky, huh?

And it's not even something we can control. It happens to us, with or without our knowledge or active participation.

Let me explain. I sat down at the computer at 9:00 p.m. I typed for a total of maybe twenty minutes, and when I looked up, it was 10:00 p.m. That means I traveled forward in time an extra forty minutes.

Conversely, if I have to watch someone else's kid, time, without me even trying, will slow down to a rate of one minute per ten minutes. This means after watching a full ten minutes of kid hyperactivity, I will look up at the clock, and see only one minute has elapsed.

When we finally fully understand this, we'll be able to make larger, more controlled jumps, which I may be able to use to improve my softball game somehow. And maybe take a longer lunch. Hopefully, we can figure out how to do it without involving someone else's kid.

5:45

I was talking to a friend who worked for a competitor once. Hey! There's no law against this!

Anyway, I was getting ready to leave, and wished him a nice day, and he said he had to work until 5:45.

5:45?

Not six, not five-thirty, but five-forty five.

He said he started work at 7:30, and worked until 5:45 every day. This didn't compute for me, and I asked if he took a half-hour lunch, or a full hour. And to my surprise, he said he gets forty-five minutes.

Who gets forty-five minutes? How goofy is this?

I can see getting an hour, a half-hour, or even fifteen minutes. But what's this forty-five minutes stuff? Nobody takes forty-five minutes.

This got me thinking about other weird timing stuff. Like who ever decided eight hours is the right number of hours to work? And how strange is it that while New York's celebrating each new year, California, allegedly part of the same country, is on an entirely different year, at least for a few more hours?

Well, okay, maybe this isn't so weird. California doesn't always play by the same rules as the rest of us.

But think about it. How can it be one year for one part of our country, and be an entirely different year in another part of the country, at the same time?

And how about those poor slobs who were unfortunate enough to be born on February 29? How would you feel if you'd been around for twenty rotations of the Earth around the sun, but only be five years old?

How weird is that?

And when would this person celebrate his or her birthday in off years? March 1 or February 28?

And what's the deal about five-minute breaks? Or ten-minute breaks?

Why can't we have a seven-minute break? Or seven and a half minutes?

Hey, I gotta go take my thirteen-minute break.

Chapter 13   Guys and God

Licorice Whips

It's Promise Keepers time again, where Christian men meet at (where else?) sporting arenas to reaffirm our commitment to God, Jesus, each other, our families, and smelling bad. It was a stroke of genius for the organizers to make sport stadiums the venue for this event, which is being held nationwide. Where else can men be more at home?

We three, Doug, Gary and I, having lost our fourth from last year (Gary's dad), who couldn't make it this year, decided to sojourn to the event in St. Louis, rather than attend the rally in Chicago or Indianapolis. We reasoned that we can better appreciate our family if we put a little distance between us.

We had three rules for the road:

#1) no potty stops;

#2) no stopping for directions;

#3) no hogging the licorice whips.

Having sworn to these rules, we three intrepid travelers jumped in the Caravan and proceeded South to St. Louis. It didn't take us long to realize that none of us had brought a map or directions. But, being men, we decided this wasn't critical. Anyway, we left plenty early because there were no kids to slow us down.

Using our **Guy Stadium Homing Instinct** we unerringly found our way to Busch Stadium, home of the baseball St. Louis Cardinals. We didn't realize that the event was actually being held in the TWA Stadium, home of the football Rams. A little later we showed up at the right stadium, tired, exhausted and with our supply of licorice whips down to fumes. We pulled into the parking lot just as we were resorting to taking big sniffs out of the bag.

The first night we witnessed an incredible, heart-lifting scene. We were milling in the milling crowd, milling around the entrance, and there, before us, were real, actual live scalpers! Promise Keepers is big time! Men want to be here! There were actually men who traveled to the Stadium, without tickets, just hoping that they could score some tickets so that they could join in spiritual revival!

The next day we were back in the filled stadium. There were excellent speakers, and we learned many things, too many to encapsulate here. There were certain messages, though, that were aimed right at my heart.

Some of the clearer messages I received were,

- Don't go into debt to purchase things meant to impress people you don't know or like.
- Don't justify yourself in the eyes of men, justify yourself in the eyes of God.
- Lead your family spiritually.
- Don't be quiet when you witness racism.
- Stop, and look people in the eyes, and see them as individuals loved equally by God.

The afternoon session was broken with a lunch break. Since we were all guys, we all knew we should leave a little early to avoid the rush. This, of course, meant that we all rushed right into the teeth of **the rush**.

Plus, it was hot out there. We snatched our food packages and then everybody sprinted for the shade. Guys bounced off each other like human bumper cars. The biggest sporting event of the weekend took place outside the stadium in the quest for shade. Finally, we all were under what shelter we could find, mostly scraggly ten-foot high saplings. We sprawled out and gobbled our food.

Did I mention that it was hot? We slucked down our lemonade and searched for more moisture. Guys were licking the condensation off their lemonade cans. Others were walking around with divining rods. I saw some guys even sucking the juice out of their lemon-scented moistwipes.

Promise Keepers was a success, personally and as an event. On the way back home, we determined that we only spent about one third of the time lost.

Being not just guys, but Guys of God armed with licorice whips, we didn't care.

Birds

While on one hand, seagulls are loud, obnoxious, squabbling creatures (kind of like city aldermen), one of the more refined and circumspect birds is the robin.

I like to walk in the woods at forest preserves, and one day drove to one near where I work. Just before I got out of the car I saw a robin, head cocked as it listened for the sound of a worm scraping through the ground. Not wanting to startle the robin, I waited in my car for it to move further away.

As I sat there, I noticed another robin, about five feet away from the first. Then I saw another, and another, all standing about five feet apart from each other, respecting each other's respective worm-listening posts.

All together, there were twenty-two robins hopping in a small clearing, with no fighting for territory, and no squabbling over disputed wormage.

Just sitting there, reveling in what nature was allowing me to see, I reflected that I enjoy watching birds, because they embody how fragile the spark of life really is. It would take very little to snuff out each little bird.

I thought of all the dead birds I've seen, babies blown out of their nests after a windy storm, or a feathery carnage after a cat-attack. And little insects, their tiny lives crushed beneath my careless feet. Each is animated by something I feel God put there, maybe a part of Himself. Maybe life is just that, a part of God that He bestows on us as a gift to His creations.

I believe in science, and I believe that we evolve; but I don't think it's just random. Chance may blow the particles together, but something gives it life. If someone were to asphyxiate, or die in some other manner that didn't harm the body, there would be a short interval where the body is lifeless, but in every other way capable of sustaining life if somehow it could be sparked again. Instead, it soon starts decomposing, to return nutrients to the earth.

Some people say God doesn't exist, because He isn't out performing little bush burnings on every corner. They say, "Show me, and I'll believe!"

However, these same people have no problem believing in wind, **even though it's invisible**, simply because they can feel it. If these same people were put in glass houses, away from the wind, for their whole lives, they probably wouldn't believe in wind!

Whenever I have trouble believing in something I just think of wind. By the way, George Burns died not so long ago at the age of one hundred years old. I saw a comic on the editorial page of the *Chicago Tribune* that showed George's arrival in heaven. And when he got there, he found that he looked just like God. I kind of like the thought of God looking like George Burns.

Voices
Another pretty clever God-invention is our voices. Almost any mother can identify her child's cry from eighty-two yards, across from a wild carnival. But think about it. Our voices are simply air being forced past a rubber-band type structure in our throat. The air vibrates this structure, creating sound waves, which are emitted from our tunnel-like mouth, and then travel around bumping into things and entering weird folds of skin on the sides of our heads, before getting translated by our own personal bongo drummer into something our brain interprets.

With all these vibrations emitting, traveling, bumping and drumming around, it's amazing how we can identify individual voices from all the sound waves bouncing around, through, and under each other.

We all have our favorite singers, and can identify one of their new songs easily, just by the sound of their voices. We can even identify someone's voice through the distortion (that your personal telemarketer sets up) and displacement of your phone.

I have a wonderful voice, but, for some reason, when I hear recorded versions of my voice, it sounds horrible. I know that can't be right. Someone, somewhere somehow is plotting against me, and have caused all recordings of my voice to come out distorted as a screeching, whining, gross kind of fingernails-on-the-chalkboard kind of wailing that would stun a PMS-enraged cigarette executive in mid attack.

Not only that, but everybody who hears my singing is in on the plot, because they all try to tell me my singing is, not only offensive, but probably illegal in most states. This is why I know cigarette companies or gun control lobbyists are involved. Because so many people have been coerced to maintain this illusion, I concluded that only an extremely well-financed organization with a very strong government lobby is funding the project.

...

It's pretty hard to shame me into doing anything (though it's not so hard to shame me out of doing something). Anyway, public opinion and the threat of the singing police slapping me into mouth cuffs, has convinced me to honor the petitions requesting that I not sing, at least until I can get lobbying outlawed.

Unsubstantiated rumor has it that one day in 1972, before I learned of the insidious plot, my vocal emissions deafened fourteen people during a rousing solo of Simon and Garfunkel's song, *Cecilia*. I don't know how much the cigarette lobby paid them, but these fourteen people carried on this deception of deafness even so far as learning and becoming adept at sign language.

Anyway, I went to Promise Keepers at the Pontiac Silverdome in 1996. Seventy thousand men went to a stadium (with no beer or football in sight!) to escape their wives and children for a two-day inspirational seminar preaching the values of family (which is easier when you are five hours away from your family), God and racial harmony.

On the second day, when it was time to feed the masses, and breaking one loaf of bread didn't work, they ordered out. They then airlifted, forklifted and spoonlifted boxes of food, and left it out in the parking lot, while issuing a bulletin that our wives had warned the organizers that we are all eating-impaired and wipe our mouths on our sleeves, so we would have to eat outside.

During the orderly excursion (with only a few non-Christian like stomping fatalities) we grabbed our food and huddled for almost three seconds, wondering whether to stand in the freezing cold or go to a nice warm van. Being guys, comfort won out.

A note here: when a guy goes to a stadium event, or gets dragged out to a mall (to hold his wife's purse and witness the demise of their Visa credit line), his single biggest thought, an actual unwritten commandment from God, should be, **"Thou shalt remember where you parked!"**

There were seventy-thousand men at this event, with probably thirty to forty thousand vehicles in the parking lots. We bee-lined right to our van, because I, as our driver, paid homage to God's commandment, and remembered that I was parked outside the East entrance, twenty-two feet north of the 'D-1' marker. There we commenced chowing.

Meanwhile, many other men were going to their vans, buses and cars, and we saw them walking by. Then we saw some of them walking by again. Then we saw them again. They split into scout parties, looking for their Dodge Caravans, Ford Windstars, space shuttles and covered wagons.

Some of them opened their lunch boxes, and started leaving bread crumb trails. One guy, near tears, scrambled to the top of a Winnebago, clutching his lunch box, and peered in all directions, wondering where he had parked. One scouting party actually found their van, but they lost their driver, who had the keys. We sat in cozy warmth, tummies filled, helplessly convulsed with laughter. We knew we shouldn't help, because God doesn't take lightly those that break His commandments. These men must serve their penance.

Later, when we were back in the stadium, they reopened the program with hymns of 69,999 deep voices joyously singing the praises of God.

All of us, minus one. Me.

I simply watched, deeply fearful of deafening 69,999 men, so they could no longer hear the heavenly words, "Play ball!," and then noticed something. In the front row, right in front of the singers, a man was standing, facing the crowd, and was noiselessly signing everything in the songs.

He was signing to fourteen men, allegedly deafened in 1972 by someone screeching the Simon and Garfunkel song, *Cecilia*. These men were signing in unison with the man. Even though they couldn't hear the songs (allegedly!), they still lifted their 'voices' to God, in the only way they could.

I realized, to my shame that I shouldn't worry about lobbyists, or the singing police, or what anyone else thinks about my singing. So I gathered my courage, took a deep breath, and valiantly made it seventy thousand singers, all singing for our god.

Soon after returning to my church, I discovered a brilliant new strategy for singing in church. I find the best loud-singing man in the church, and move right in front of him. That way he drowns me out. There's also the added benefit that many might think it's actually me singing that well.

God

The whole subject of God, Jesus and the Holy Spirit has given me tremendous cause to think. I was born to a Presbyterian and Catholic, who raised our family with no religion, rather than simply picking between these two divergent sects, who have had their shares of wars over the centuries. As a result, I didn't know what to believe.

I learned in high school cross-country that I was religious, and definitely believe in a higher being. I'd be panting my way through the second mile, and find myself praying I'd make it through the race. I wouldn't consciously decide to pray, I'd just find myself doing it. I know God answered me in every single race, because **I'm still alive today.** So I searched for religion, because I knew there was a God I had to discover.

Back in college I had a psychology class that started at 8:00 in the morning (if there was ever a class that shouldn't start at 8:00, it's psychology!). There I struck up a friendship with an associate pastor who, upon learning of my search for religion, willingly met with me before class to discuss the subject. You have to know me to realize how remarkable it was that I would go early to an 8:00 class. We used to meet in the cafeteria, drink coffee, and just talk.

I became a big coffee drinker in college for the same reason most guys do. Because the Sororities were selling coffee and bagels in the halls every morning.

During our discussions, I learned just how splintered religions really are. My friend honestly felt if you didn't believe in **exactly his way** you wouldn't go to heaven. That makes you want to come running, huh?

I asked him why so many people, who weren't so lucky to be born into a Christian home that practiced his particular Christianity, are doomed forever simply because they were unfortunate enough to have been born in China, India, or New Jersey. He responded, saying that everybody has a chance at some time in his or her life to be converted, and that's why there are Missionaries all over the world, including China.

So I popped him my Big Question, asking, "What would you do if you led the righteous life, went to heaven, and when you got there you found billions of Chinese sitting around Buddha? And that you were given access to heaven, even though you were mistaken, because you are honest, righteous and good."

He simply couldn't or wouldn't comprehend this, and never really answered my question. He also felt that Catholics and other similar, but different, religious people, would not make it into heaven unless they converted to his true faith.

Personally, I think most religions are a lot closer than people think, and the differences are in comprehension and perception, not reality. That's why I'm happy that Promise Keepers has been teaching this same thing.

I went to a Catholic church for a while, and occasionally go to Catholic functions, and found that their beliefs are pretty much the same as Presbyterianism. It's just that they get more into the trappings, and revere each religious icon to a degree no one else does. They worship Mary, the cross, the cup, the Pope, the Saints, the door to the church, the Little Drummer Boy's drumstick, etc. The other Christian religions feel these are sacred, too, but not to the same extent.

[Warning: my wife Sandy hates the following two paragraphs. If you don't have a sense of humor or ridiculousness, then what are you doing reading this book? Oops, I mean, skip these paragraphs. And remember, we were made in God's image, which proves He has a sense of humor, so it's okay with Him that I do this]

How did they break the news to Joseph? Did God appear as a burning bush, and say, "Joe, We have to have a talk. I've got good news and bad news. The good news is you don't have to worry about Mary having a period for a few months..." How do you think you would have taken this kind of blessing, huh? Joseph really deserves a lot more attention.

Anyway, back to the Holy Trinity. But first, I want to compliment Joseph on his attitude about the immaculate conception. He took the whole thing much better than I would have, and displayed an admirable amount of restraint and support. Most people think more of and revere Mary more than they do Joseph, and I don't think he is really getting his just due. He's the one, after all, who threw a ball around with boy Jesus, even when he knew He was someone else's kid. I think if there's some Christian church out there that's feeling kind of aimless, they might consider erecting a statue of Joseph and bringing him up on a par with Mary.

Also, and **I must stress, repeat, I must stress and I really mean it,** I am not suggesting anything about Jesus when I tell you about a word I looked up the other day. Somehow, in the course of a conversation, we started wondering what a female bastard is called. Everyone knows a bastard is a boy born out of wedlock. We were wondering if a female would be a 'bastardess' or 'bastardette.' Anticipating that you would want to know, I consulted with Webster, and learned that bastard is the correct form of address for either a male or female born out of wedlock.

...

I keep going off on tangents, huh?

Once, back when my daughter was eight, I was helping her prepare for Communion, and I started thinking about how she prays at night. I'll listen, and sometimes she prays to God, and sometimes she prays to Jesus, so I wondered which one you should address your prayers to. And how come no one prays to the Holy Ghost? Someone, somewhere must surely pray, "Dear Holy Ghost: please bless my mother and father and roller skates, and thank you..."

We went to a Communion class, so I asked the teacher to whom you should address your prayers, God or Jesus. He replied that you should say, "Dear God, in Jesus' name." I think he skirted my question, plus he's still leaving the Holy Ghost out. Maybe it's the whole ghost thing. Most people still get a little spooked when they think of ghosts, so it's understandable that they'd be a little nervous.

I think the proper prayer should start, "Dear God, in Jesus' name, in the presence of the Holy Spirit, and after the prophets and saints, etc." so everyone gets their dues. Maybe just run a credits screen in your head like the ones after movies.

I realized, that personally, I don't say 'Dear God' or 'Dear Jesus.' I figure the only entity who's going to hear what I say in my own mind doesn't need me to address Him in any particular way.

And if I did, I'd better add 'Mister.'

Evolution

When you start doubting the presence of God, you need look no further than your own nose. When we think of evolution, we recall scientific theories that we may eventually lose our little toes, since we don't really use them to eat. And some scientists think if we returned to the water, where we would weigh less (though we would not lose mass), we would eventually develop webbed hands and feet.

If this is true, then why have our noses gotten *bigger* even as we rely *less* on our sense of smell? We use our noses less than monkeys do, yet ours are far more pronounced. I've seen some specimens of human honker, which if truly indicative of olfactory ability, would allow its bearer to surpass my basset hound in foraging through his kibbles for the bits.

Therefore, I believed at first that our noses' evolution was divinely inspired. However, upon reflection, and considering how the nose is a convenient doorway for germs, and further how our noses are precisely aligned to keep rain out of our sinus cavities, I had to rethink this. Consider how a monkey's nostrils face outward to present a wider range in their hunt for food, while ours face downward, since most of our food is thrust right under it. And some people consider the angle just right for the proper insertion of a finger.

Evolution or not? You decide.

...

If George Burns, I mean, God, agreed to sit down with me (in a metaphysical sort of way), and conduct a direct verbal question and answer session, I have many questions I would like to pose. Among them include the following:

Did You ever have any brothers, sisters or parents?

Is Jesus going to remain an only Son?

Why did You create telemarketers, and how can we get rid of them if they become addicted to the theme song to the cartoon, 'Josie and the Pussycats'?

What is the meaning of Life?

How high are the vollyball nets in Heaven?

If You wanted to, could you just wipe out Hell?

How does a crab have sex?

What comes after the end of the Universe?

How do You cure the common cold, and when are You going to let us in on the secret?

But if He is kind of impatient, because maybe He's suffering from a bad cold or something, or if he doesn't think my puny mind can handle more than one question, I'd be happy to limit my interview to one question, which would be ...

Where did you come from?

...

JUST SOME THOUGHTS ON GOD:

God tinkers with His creations. This is 'evolution.'

God is a mathematician, everything fits together in a numeric way. There are two hydrogens for every oxygen in water, the formula never waivers.

God is the consummate artist. Who can imagine a better color for the sky, or a sunset, grass or flowers? Even mud is the right color.

God wants us to think, and He gives us much to think about.

People wonder how God can see all, yet they do not question how a computer can process millions of bits of information in a second.

God likes puzzles, and creates the most intricate on a genetic level.

Who says creationism and evolution cannot co-exist? A day for God is not the same as a day for His creations.

God has a sense of humor. Proof is that He made me.

Feeding the Poor

I went to a Chicago Bulls basketball game when You-Know-Who was still playing for them. Yep, John Paxson.

My friends and I met before the game at a restaurant that would allow us to leave all of our vehicles and go in one car. This restaurant, which will remain nameless (the Rosebud), specializes in giving you enough food to feed you, half the population of Rhode Island, and twenty-two robins. In other words, almost enough to fill up my dog.

When you're done gorging, without even asking, they pack the remainder of your dinner in a U-haul to tow away when you leave. We gorged. They packed. We left.

Jerry drove, and we lurched towards the Stadium. When we got there the parking was almost capacity, and the game was ready to start. Since Jerry owed season's tickets, he offered to park while the rest of us went in.

As he pulled away, Glenn noticed, to his dismay, that he was still holding the package full of his leftovers. We all laughed as he stood there, a lost look on his face.

Still chuckling, we turned to walk the last hundred yards to the Stadium, when a man, bundled against the cold, approached, asking if we had any money to spare. I think the people who beg for a living (and some actually make a decent living), when they don't really need the money, have ruined it for the people who really do desperately need a helping hand. We all become sort of jaded, and don't even trust the one who is really in need. Nobody wants to help support someone's drug or drinking habits, so how can you know?

But I knew if this guy was really hungry, he would appreciate food, so I nudged Glenn, and suggested he fork (sorry) the food package over to the man. He did, and a real smile of job crossed the man's face. It was genuine and immediate proof of his need.

I know this doesn't really seem like an expansive gesture. I have strong feelings about charity, and believe everyone should be generous to those who cannot (as opposed to will not) support themselves temporarily. It is difficult to find the right charities that guarantee giving what you give to the proper recipients, without too much ending up in the wrong place (look at the scandals at the United Way).

Once, on a cold blustery day, I was driving north on the Dan Ryan Expressway, heading out of Chicago, and I got off at an exit not too far north of the city. As you exit, you drive down a ramp for about a hundred yards to a light, where you can turn east or west.

I was sitting at this light, about six cars from the intersection, when I noticed a slim woman of about forty holding a sign and walking car to car, stopping at each driver's side window. She was pretty calm after the first car, but got more agitated at the second car, and was very upset by the time she got to the third. She was yelling at the driver of this car, who left his window up, and ignored her. She was extremely upset, and I couldn't imagine why. I couldn't hear any of what she was saying, and right then the light changed, and we started moving forward.

When the traffic started moving, she turned and walked back towards the intersection, and as I drove slowly by her I looked over to see if I could figure what she was so upset about. She didn't look up, but now I could see that the cardboard sign she was carrying said, "I need money to feed my kids." Up closer, she looked a little older and more worn, dressed in a light jacket that couldn't have done much to keep her warm. She had a hopeless look on her face that couldn't be faked.

I turned left at the light, and the traffic forced me along. As I drove, I thought about the faceless people I help with other charities, and my suspicions about how much really gets to them. If she were really trying to feed children today, and was doing as poorly as her frustrations suggested, I had to believe she wasn't just trying to get a fix or a buzz.

But to be sure, I drove a few blocks until I saw a grocery store. Though I was on my way to a business meeting, I felt I had to do this. I went into the store and bought three bags of groceries, including bread, canned meats, canned fruits and vegetables, milk and juice.

I drove back to the intersection, hoping she would still be there, but also kind of nervous that she would be there too. She wasn't. I drove around the block, and came down the road again, still not seeing her. I redoubled back, and then I saw her, walking down the sidewalk, hunched against the wind.

Fortunately, there was a place I could pull up, and I stopped right next to her. I opened the door, and shouted, "Hello, hello?" She heard me, and turned around. Up close, I saw she was more worn than she had looked, with deeper lines on her face. Her hands were chapped and red from the cold. She was definitely out there because she had nowhere else to go.

I said, pulling the bags out of the car, "I saw you back there and want to help. Hopefully, this will help you." And I handed her the bags.

The look on her face made me want to drive up and down with bags of groceries for everyone. She really needed help, and this would help give her a few days of lessened concern.

I've given directly to people before. Usually I try to give some kind of food, because I know what they will do with it. You always see people begging in the streets of downtown Chicago. You never know what their real needs are, or what they do with donations. Well-off pedestrians bustle by them, immune to the sight and sounds. So do I, sometimes.

But sometimes not.

Audience

Have you ever gone to church or to a seminar? Do you just sit in your seat in the anonymous protection of the audience, shut off your mind, and wait to be entertained? Do you stare vacuously at the speaker with your brain waves slowing to a vapid nothing? Well, don't do it!! Do you realize how frightening this is to the speaker? All he sees are these blank stares. He needs to know that he is reaching you.

I have given several speeches and taught some classes, and take it from me, you audience members need to take lessons in how to be responsive audiences! You need to learn how to do the encouraging smile, and put the entertained sparkle in your eyes. You need to murmur your appreciation at the most poignant parts of the speech.

I was in church the other day and the pastor was talking about the fear of death. He said that the only thing that scares people more than the thought of dying, is the thought of speaking in public. I don't think he's right though. I learned that when you take a speech class, you are told to imagine the audience in their underwear.

Ever since I heard this, my biggest fear is being in an audience.

Life-saving

I hope I didn't throw you too much when I said I used to teach classes. Actually, the classes I taught were swimming, first aid, CPR and lifesaving.

Once, I was teaching lifesaving at a community college. I was imagining all of the students in their underwear, not a far cry from what they were actually wearing, and I decided to use an attention-grabbing scheme (AGS) to get their attention and wipe out their vapid stares. So I had my assistant, a pretty young college coed, jump in the pool and pretend she was drowning.

My class of students were all police, EMT's, fireman and other husky, hirsute, *Home Improvement* Tim Taylor sort of brutes. I was standing in front of them in my Speedos (I utilize more fabric nowadays), and was straddling about six kinds of lifesaving devices that would all work without entering the water.

I turned around, pointed out my assistant, a huge monster grossing all of one hundred-ten pounds, flailing in the water, and turned back to the Cro-Magnons in front of me on the bleachers and shouted, "She's drowning, can anybody save her?!"

They all stared at me stupidly from beneath their unibrows, as the message worked its way through dense brain matter.

Finally, a Darth Vader-type leaped to his feet, and in the best Canadian Mounty style, proclaimed, "I'll save her!!"

He valiantly vaulted over the lifesaving equipment I had put there for his use, and was soon stroking manfully through the water to his victim, amid the themesong to *Baywatch*.

Yeah, as you probably figured out, she clobbered him.

By the time he got her to shore he had a bloody nose and a slew of gouges shaped like a woman's talons, er nails.

Chapter 14 Guys and telemarketers

Telemarketer

If you remember, earlier I wrote about the sand tiger shark and its double uterus. Another similar animal developed this double uterus phenomenon with differing results. The 'sucker-faced' telemarketer, as opposed to its close relation, the 'yellow-bellied' telemarketer, also has two uteri. The difference is, rather than eating each other, the sucker-faced telemarketers eat their way out of their eggs, multiply again while still in the uterus, and immediately force themselves to birth (often after selling five thousand dollars worth of siding to the mother).

After emerging, they crawl, leaving a slimy snail-like trail, to the nearest phone, and slither into the receiver. Waiting until darkness, they begin eating parts of the phone receiver and transmitter. Afterwards, they attach themselves to the empty shell of the receiver to digest and begin an amazing transformation. They regurgitate some of their food, and begin to spin a webbed cocoon. Within ten minutes, there is a hard shell covering them, as nature begins to work its miracle on their bodies.

Finally, almost thirty minutes later, a split appears down the cocoon, as the nymph-telemarketer emerges from the interior of the cocoon. First, the antennae peeks out, and a scaly claw reaches forward, and pulls the opening wider. As it opens, the face of the eyeless telemarketer pushes through, dragging its phone directory.

What emerges looks like an enormous pair of pursed lips, which begin to widen like a mouth opening, or butterfly's wings spreading to dry. Continuing to spread open the 'lips,' until they are shaped like a wide, shallow cone, the beast pushes out of the cocoon, and maneuvers its cone to the ear piece of the receiver, and fastens itself securely.

The tail of the telemarketer, attached by a wire-like body, slides down the handle of the phone, connecting with the transmitter in the mouthpiece of the phone. They then connect their neuro-impulse antennae to the phone's circuits and ringer; and, while still under cover of dark, write their contracts with *Time-Life Books* and other marketing giants, to begin activation of their new phone-selves.

The only way you can fight this is constantly change your number, because this temporarily blocks their neuro-impulses. Once their impulses are set, it takes longer to grow new ones than it did to create the original, which was done while their antennae were still soft and pliable after first leaving the cocoon. I also recommend hanging up the phone sharply, as it shakes them to senselessness lasting up to an hour.

Finally, although some telemarketers are developing a resistance, recent studies have shown that singing the theme song to the cartoon "Josie and the Pussycats" has a longer staying effect on these creatures.

More Telemarketers
There are three things I really want to know the answers to. I know I pass myself along as a handy-with-the-tools kind of guy, who can also make up almost any plausible explanation, but there are some things that I just can't fathom.

First of all, who ever decided that people would want their waist and inseam size emblazoned on the outside of a pair of jeans? I don't know about you, but it amuses me to check out the girth and squattiness of anyone I'm standing behind who's wearing a pair of Levi's. I'm sure you look, too (don't lie, people actually buy *The National Enquirer*). I think this is the true reason people try to squeeze into jeans that are too small.

The next question is why auto makers install ashtrays in cars. Smokers simply fling their butts out the window (to be gawked at by the nearest male) when they are done smoking. The only thing that goes into ashtrays is gum, change, and the infrequent ashes from a smoking passenger, who will only use ashtrays in someone's car other than his own.

And finally, why do telemarketers only call during the reruns of *Home Improvement* that runs up here every weekday at 6:00 PM on Fox Channel 32 (which we get on channel 12 in my house)? They never call during dinner, or when I'm putting the kids in bed or helping them with homework. They only call during the one time I allow myself to relax.

I hate telemarketers.

Even more telemarketers

Over the years I've considered several strategies for dealing with telemarketers, and have to let you in on the one that proved better than any of them. I tried all the other ones, like asking them for their home numbers so that I could call them at their houses during their free time. I also told them I'd buy their stuff if they bought something from me. And the old 'I'd love to, does it matter if my bankruptcy isn't discharged yet?'

But all these pale in comparison to the hideous torture I finally conceived for them, because I hate them for calling during reruns of *Home Improvement*. What I would do is race for the phone to pick it up before the answering machine kicks in. I listen to the first earnest pleading from the individual who could, if they chose, do anything rather than interrupt *Home Improvement*. And what kind of person would rather call me than be watching *Home Improvement* at his or her home? I digress.

As I listen to Mr. or Mrs. Telemarketer, my kids, who had been racing behind me, because they are involved in this plot, say in unison, "And a one, and a two..." and then launch into a rousing chorus of the theme song to the cartoon, "Josie and the Pussycats." I hold the phone near to these tender children of mine as they emotionally belt out this kid's anthem, while I revel in the thought of the look that must surely be on the telemarketers's face.

After two verses, which I know by heart, I listen to the receiver for signs of life, and carefully hang up, not wanting to disturb the thrall the telemarketer must surely be experiencing.

It stopped most of the calls, except from the folks at Time-Life, who must have been addicted to my kids' singing.

Now that my kids are getting older, I've started substituting them with my basset and cat, who belt out a rousing rendition of *Born Free.*

A final word on telemarketers.

In January 2003, the FTC (short for Full Time Competency, or Free The Chickens) ruled that....(hey, pay attention!)... people who wanted to eat dinner **in their own houses** could henceforth (important legal term) sign up for a national Do Not Call list.

Yeah, baby!

Do you get what that would mean?! No phone calls during dinner! Nobody calling while you're slorking down spaghetti and meatballs, using your own phone to convince you to transfer your money to their wallets.

And think what this would mean to your dog! Intensified begging, without the distraction of telephone interruptions. No worries about getting his tail tromped on as your teenager breaks Olympic hurdle records on her way to a ringing phone. Canine peace of mind.

But then doom struck.

A judge (defined as someone whose job it is to make sure murderers get off on mere technicalities, real minor stuff. I mean, seriously, what's so bad about a little illegal search and seizure?)...

Anyway, this judge said that the Federal government did not have the authority to do this.

What?! The Federal government doesn't have the right to protect us?

Yep, that's what I said, protect us.

Because that's what a telemarketer call is, isn't it? An assault.

Think about it. When a telemarketer calls, isn't it an attack on your peace, and, dare I say it, your actual health? Doesn't your blood go into systolic gyrations? Don't you grind your teeth to nubs? Don't you feel like reaching through the phone and strangling the telemarketer with his own tongue?

Not only that, but they invite themselves into your house, unwanted and unannounced, pushing you with ferocity not seen since your teenaged daughter begged you for a belly button piercing. (Yeah, I'm a normal Dad. I counted to ten and said "NO!" before hitting two.)

So the FTC stepped in, and said, "No way. A guy should be able to sit at his own dinner table, surrounded by his begging children and adoring dog, er, um.. I mean adoring children and begging dog, and consume chicken pot pie without some schmuck barging in with telephonic interruption, trying to get you to switch to MCI."

I was so happy I cheered. And it wasn't even a sporting event!

So, like millions, I happily signed up, and waited anxiously for some telemarketer to screw up and call me, so that I could sue him; and then here come the judge, here come the judge, watch out baby, here come the judge.

It seems like this ruling interfered with telemarketers' constitutional right to make money. An intrusion on Free Enterprise.

Oh, boo, hoo, hoo!

Is arresting a dope dealer interfering with his right to make money in a free enterprise system? Or is it restraint of trade when you apprehend a burglar?

Telemarketers don't have the right to invade your privacy!!!!

The people who have rights???!!!! Us!!!!!!!!!! Leave us alone!!!!! Let us eat!!!!!

I gotta go, my ! key is getting kinda hot.

Chapter 15 Guys and world events

Contrary to thought, guys spend a lot of time watching the news and thinking about the world around us. Then we get scared, and turn on the game. But here's

Expensive Cuppa Joe
The fallout continues from the multi-million dollars awarded by a jury to Stella Liebeck, who sued McDonald's restaurants after she had dumped hot coffee on her own lap; despite the valiant efforts of a pimply teenaged McDonald's employee, who tried to leap to her rescue amid the musical strains of the theme song to *Baywatch*.

A note to all you attorneys out there, don't ever pick me to be a juror in one of these cases. No way do I believe that I should pay $2.00 for my Big Mac, instead of $1.99, just because some lady doesn't know coffee is hot! However, I'd like to have been a male mosquito on the wall and heard how they rationalized this. I'm sure it sounded something like this:

Juror #1: "I definitely think McDonald's was grossly negligent here! After all, they named their cocoa 'Hot Chocolate.' This implied they knew the risks!"

Juror #3: "What are you saying? That they should call the coffee '**Hot** Coffee'?"

Juror #2: "Yeah! And Big Macs should be called 'Sloppy, Warm Big Macs' so people are warned that you could get stuff all over yourselves, causing great emotional distress and dry-cleaning bills."

Juror #7: "Are you implying that people don't have the sense to know coffee is made from adding steaming, boiling water to ground-up coffee beans? And that you get your best coffee when you make and maintain the coffee at 176 degrees or more?"

At this point, the other jurors jump on and pummel Juror #7, because the judge had instructed them in their jury deliberations to throw common sense out the window, just as had happened in the *O.J. Simpson Murder Variety Show*.

Anyway, I was in a Mexican Restaurant the other day, and personally experienced fallout from the McDonald's trial. Prior to taking our order, our server brought out a basket of tortilla chips and two bowls of salsa. I told the server to give the mild salsa to the kids and give me the hot. Instead she hesitated, cleared her throat, and apologetically said, "I'm sorry, but we don't serve the hot salsa anymore."

She didn't say why, but I knew. Yes, I knew.

(In a related development, McDonald's announced plans to add cold Mc-Coffee and luke-warm Mc-Coffee to their Mc-menu for the stirring-impaired.)

Advertising

Imagine this, if you can. Weight Watchers, the huge, uh, sorry, big corporate giant, assigns the bulk, uh, er, most of their advertising to a new Ad company, whose first order of business is, "Who should we pick as company spokesperson?" I kind of imagine the conversation sounded something like this:

Ad-guy # 1: "How about Rosie O'Donnell, she's overweight."

Ad-guy # 2, dabbing some Brill Crème into his hair: "Nah, we can't use her, she actually doesn't mind being heavy."

Ad-gal # 4, sipping sparkling water: "Yeah, and she'd expect us to put kids meal toys in each box."

Ad-guy # 3, while simultaneously entering a lunch date in his palm pilot: "Oprah would be great, she's always fighting the Battle of the Bulge."

Ad-gal # 4 again, dabbing her chin delicately with a cloth napkin: "Way too expensive, we need someone cheap."

Ad-guy #2, wishing he was alone so that he could navigate his nasal passages to remove a likely clog: "Hey, you want cheap? I can give you cheap!"

And a spokesperson was born, Monica Lewinsky.

Remember her?

Cigar/President/nasty stuff.

What the heck were they thinking?!? This is worse than Nike (motto: "Our spokesperson makes more than all of our assembly line people make put together) hiring Michael Jordan to hawk their wares. Worse than supermodel Kathy Ireland introducing a clothing line at K Mart.

What next?

How about a cutlery company hiring OJ Simpson or Loretta Cuttit, I mean Bobbitt, to be their spokesperson? Or maybe boxing promoter Don (I have never been convicted of embezzling) King could represent accountant giant Arthur Anderson. Or maybe you can imagine Newt Gingrich selling muzzles, former President Clinton hawking Trojan condoms, or mebbe a line of Charlie Manson bibles?

How would you like to see Bill Gates representing a loan company? Imagine, Super Rich Geeky Guy telling you, "Wouldn't you like to consolidate your debt so you can pay your bills?" This kind of stuff just doesn't make sense, but advertising companies keep match-making ridiculous spokespeople with ill-fitting companies using, "hey, you've heard of me" reasoning.

Back in college, before I had any respect for myself, my major was pre-law, which I swiftly switched to advertising once I started hearing the volumes of attorney jokes that proliferate our culture. (Example: What's the difference between a dead skunk in the middle of the road, and a dead attorney in the middle of the road? Answer: There are skid marks in front of the skunk.)

I already have two kids, a dog, a cat, a bird, and a receded hairline, so I don't need this kind of abuse. And I'd never heard a joke putting down advertising people.

So I changed my major to advertising, visions of using my creative juices to their ultimate, um, uh, ... chemistry... , uh, yeah... that's what I mean. So I designed billboards, wrote commercials, developed marketing surveys, and drew storyboards earnestly in preparation for my chosen profession. And then, in my Senior year, too late to change, I learned the truth. Advertising is, ...

GAAAK!!!!!

.....almost as despicable and disreputable as lawyers!

Advertising guys scurrying down the halls clutching ad copies to their chests, are almost as sordid as poorly dressed attorneys skittering down halls of justice. So I crept through my senior year, mumbling quickly and changing the subject whenever anyone asked what I was studying, trying to trick people into thinking I was taking basket-weaving or Phys Ed, so they would think maybe I was an athlete or something instead. Then, whenever I applied for a job I simply wrote I was a marketing major and smudged the ink whenever anyone pushed the point.

Boy, this confession is good for the soul.

Anyway, I buried this dark secret, but I still cringe whenever I see really vapid advertising, which pretty much covers everything out there.

But there is still hope for advertising, because, after all, there was Dave. Remember him. The owner of Wendy's restaurants, the regular guy who melts the ice at a hockey game when he sneaks in with a spicy Wendy's chicken. There's also the Menards guy, flashing his lopsided grin at the end of each commercial.

And me.

I'm available.

Do you hear that, advertising people? Consider using someone like me! A normal guy. A guy who once admired you, wanted to be one of you!

Nuts.

By the way, what can you tell when you find an advertising agent buried up to his neck in sand? They ran out of sand!

Sandy
I don't want to get into trouble here, but I figured out some of our war strategy. I was watching the whole Iraq thing, and heard about a sandbag-making machine that by itself would save forty soldiers' worth of labor making sandbags.

That's when it occurred to me. We went to war in Iraq, because we knew that when we shipped all of our materiel and stuff over to Iraq, we wouldn't have to bring sand! There was a desert already there, just for us.

Yeah, baby!

I know. You scoff.

But, let's look at Russia. We could have gone to war with them any number of times during the Cold War. But you know why we didn't? You got it. Ice. We didn't want to load sandbags with ice, because we'd have problems with the Sandbag Union. It just wouldn't pass OSHA requirements. So we put off war, ignoring every slight and provocation from the Soviet Regime.

Cuba? No desert, no war. Coincidence? I think not.

There also wasn't any sand in the former Yugoslavia. So, instead of landing troops, who would have needed sandbags, we just flew overhead, never parking our rumps in harm's way.

And check out Somalia. Did we go there? Yep, you bet we did. Can you say, 'Sahara'?

That's why France is safe. You can't fill a sandbag with arrogance.

Flags
The sign on the front door at Walmart said it all, "Sorry, we don't have any flags." This was the third store I had attempted in my search, which was starting to resemble a scavenger hunt. At

one of the stores, the lady just shrugged helplessly when I asked if she knew anywhere that might have them in stock.

Where are all the flags?

Easy, they were already waving, proudly and defiantly … from the tops of buildings, the backs of motorcycles, front porches, at half-mast in front of government and civilian buildings, draped from bridges, mailboxes, peoples' desks. Everybody broke open their Fourth of July wardrobes.

September 11, 2001 marked a turning point in American patriotism, waking up a mood and a feeling that had been dormant for too long.

The horrific, cowardly action taken against unarmed civilians by demented fruitcakes, who believe the only way they can get to heaven is by killing innocent people, drew Americans together like nothing else in our generation.

People flocked to blood banks, a river of money and materials flowed into the United Way, Red Cross, and other charitable organizations. Americans, generous in spirit, opened their hearts and pocketbooks to show support and unity, rallying to New York's plight in every conceivable way.

But there's another flag we raised, in spirit if nothing else. Remember the "Don't Tread On Me" flag from the 1700's? The one with the rattlesnake on it? Well, I think this flag should fly right under the Stars and Stripes, as a warning to those so-called terrorists who think they can cow the American spirit.

There's something new for these rogues to be considering, because America showed the resolve to strike back, forcibly and against those who support and shelter them. Something to think about, next time, before they attack our populace.

And I think it's time to rename 'terrorists.' We aren't terrified … Rather, mixed with the grief, sorrow and pride, is a strong, almost overriding sense of anger.

Terrified?

Hardly

President Collection Agency

I'm sure by now you've heard about the unfortunate Superbowl incident where singer Janet Jackson accidentally tore off Justin Timberlake's pants, revealing that metrosexual's leopard skin thong underwear to the horror of eighty-eight million, nine hundred ninety nine thousand nine hundred and ninety nine viewers.

Never mind that his pants just 'happened' to be held together by Velcro.

Never mind that he didn't pull away when she tugged at his crotch.

Never mind that there was a little smiley face on the business end of the, um, bulge.

It was an accident. They promised. No cross-counts. Stick a needle in their I, er, I mean 'myself,' er, I mean 'eye'.

A troubling accident, but not as troubling as considering the one person who missed it. That person was, yep, you guessed it, President, George 'Dubya' Bush. The guy who promised to clean up America, make it safe and wholesome, and evil-doer free.

So, there he was, in the Elliptical Office, during the most-watched event of the entire day, napping through Half-time. And worse, he slept through an event that no self-respecting guy would miss!!

What's this alertness say for his other business?

'His other business' you ask?

Yeah, his other business.

The Presidency?

No, not that business. The other business. The collection agency.

Collection agency?

Yep. You didn't hear? As a recent *Trib* article discovered, the President recently learned that an oil company may have overcharged the United States $61 million for fuel sent for our invasion, I mean, liberation of Iraq. The evil-doer-fighting President vowed to contact the company and demand that they repay the money.

(Ignore that the company just happens to be his own Vice-President's former company, ... who just happened to win a 'no-bid' contract … and ignore that we are buying gasoline, … at inflated prices, no less…, and shipping it to all the way to Iraq, a country rich in oil.)

Imagine the phone call.

"Hello, Kellogg, Brown & Root."

"Hi, may I talk to your accounts-payable department," Dubya asks, tugging at his cowboy hat.

"Sure, may I tell them who's calling?"

"President George Dubya Bush."

"Yes, sir, hold on please while I connect you to that department."

"Hello, Accounts Payable," a clerk answers

"Hi, this is President George Bush, of the George Bush Collection Agency. Our records say you over-charged the U.S. by, um, … how much is that again?" he asks somebody in his office. "Oh, I see, okay, sixty one million dollars," he finishes.

"Sixty one million dollars?" asks the accounts payable clerk. "Okay, let me see here."

There's some clicking on the keyboard. The President takes a sip of carbonated water, and softly burps.

Then the clerk says, "Oh, here it is, you're right, there was a double-billing. Our mistake. We'll issue a credit memo."

"Well, okay then," the President says, satisfied.

He hangs up, and looks at a list. "Okay, let's see. Who's next?"

Yep, it's good to know that our leaders are awake for us. Willing to correct wrongs, fight evil-doers,… and keep us safe from metrosexuals flashing smiley-face leopard skin thongs at Half-time.

What? A breast?

But Justin doesn't …

Oh.

Janet? Well, okay then.

Baghdad-Bob

Have you ever seen a magic show?

Watched illusionists work their craft, making women and tigers disappear?

Well, you know who's got them beat?

The US Army, that's who.

Huh?

Let me explain. Do you remember Muhammed Saheed al-Sahaf?

Of course you do.

Good old Baghdad-Bob. The Iraqi Minister of Information during the Iraq war. He became so popular in the United States, that the only people looking for him harder than the US army were David Letterman's people.

How can we forget him, the author of…

- "…they have started to commit suicide under the walls of Baghdad. We will encourage them to commit more suicides quickly."
- "We have them surrounded in their tanks."
- "We will welcome them with bullets and shoes."

Shoes?

Of course, my wife will tell you that a Norm-shoe is pretty darn lethal. Good thing the army trains for gas warfare.

Back to my point.

The US army performed one of the most amazing illusions ever. And I can't tell the deed as well as good old, Baghdad-Bob, so let's hear it in his own words…

"They're not even (within) 100 miles (of Baghdad). They are not in any place. …This is an illusion … they are trying to sell to the others an illusion."

This, despite the fact that dust from our tanks was swirling around him.

Could David Copperfield do this? Hide an entire army?

No way. It wouldn't even matter how many scantily assistants were out there trying to divert your attention.

All of this reminded me of watching C-Span back during the investigations of cigarette companies, and remember catching a scene of a gaggle of cigarette corporation chief executives raising their right hands, and swearing an oath to Congress that they do not believe cigarettes to be addictive. I'm willing to take them at their word, since, after all, they were under oath and just stating their personal beliefs. Following though, are some of their less-publicized beliefs:

- High cholesterol, by clogging your arteries, is actually good for you, because your heart gets exercise as it works harder.
- Strokes are good for you because they allow half of your brain to rest.
- Telemarketers are simply looking out for your best interests
- Drug-induced comas enable you to improve yourself through meditation.
- Cancer is good for stimulating your nerve endings.

Hell is a nice place, because you can light up a cigarette without a match.

True Story:

I was in a Marshall Fields department store once, and saw an elderly lady walking down the aisle.

Not so unusual, especially for Fields, huh?

But was unusual was that she was wearing an oxygen mask hooked up to a portable air tank on wheels, which she pulled behind her.

It was shocking and sad to see her in that state.

Later, as I was leaving the store, there was an old lady that looked a lot like her outside. Except she didn't have an air tank.

She was smoking a cigarette.

I did a double-take, and there, sure enough, tucked in the corner behind a column, was her air tank.

There are some smokers at work, who take smoke breaks together. They call themselves "The Cemetery Club."

The Butterfly Ballet

Remember the whole election fiasco down in Florida during the Bush/Gore fight? It got ugly. Stories and rumors were flying, splattering windshields below with party-line blood and gore.

Speaking of Gore, he conceded, then reneged on his concession. Jessie Jackson declared he would personally fly to supervise the recount. Ex-President Jimmy Carter got involved, because he always gets involved with countries that don't know how to hold elections. The world held its breath, and all eyes were focused on Florida, and its 26 Electoral College votes.

Imagine that, a couple dozen college coeds deciding the fate of the entire nation.

At first, I had no fears. At least, until the story broke about Palm Beach, and the now infamous "butterfly'" ballot. You see, many of those Florida voters were retirees, **the most experienced voters in the United States!**

So how could such an experienced bunch screw up??!!

I thought our fate was in the capable hands of the same people who led us successfully through the fifties, sixties and seventies, with a long lifetime of life experience to help them decide which man should lead us into the 21st Century.

I thought we had nothing to fear. They'd surely whip those college kids into shape, right?

Yep, I called that wrong, didn't I?

What did we learn from all this? Maybe nothing, except the realization that our votes actually count for something. Over 100 million people voted in that Presidential election, and it all came down to a few hundred votes in a smallish city, in the corner of the country.

But those people in Palm Beach found out, that sometimes, it's the few, and the little things, that really make the difference between winning and losing.

On a final note, from now on, whenever you vote, you will see huge signs near the voting booths in Florida. Signs vital to the people down there.

Warning voters that McDonald's coffee is hot.

Orange Juice

By the way, I know that this is old news, but we have to talk about it, since the murderer is still at-large. Good thing we have an ex-football player available to hunt down the culprits. Anyway, the real tragedy in the O.J. Simpson Murder and Variety Show, Part II (the civil trial), which awarded millions of mostly uncollectible dollars to Ronald Goldman's family (which is urgently needed, so they can continue to purchase large quantities of his father's mustache wax), is that O.J. will be deprived of much needed capital that he urgently needs to continue his search for the real killer or killers of his ex-waiter.

"His ex-**waiter**?," you say?! "but I thought he was after his ex-wife?"

Nay, the truth of the matter is that O.J. was served some really bad O.J., this after an inordinate wait for his insolent waiter. And if you're O.J., in a hurry so you can limp through the nearest airport looking for a car rental, any delay can trigger homicidal ex-football player rage.

And if he really did do it, there are many better ways to penalize a waiter for the poor service that precipitated the carnage. For example, reduce his tip, or tip him with pocket change. Or better yet, just bring a bunch of three-year olds with you to eat the next day. You don't have to stalk him and ruin much of your own life and your expensive Bruno Madagascar loafers. Though, I guess in O.J.'s case, he saw a clear opportunity to kill two birds with one stone, since his ex-wife just happened to be available during his post-eating, poor-service killing frenzy.

I also think O.J. owes a debt of gratitude to the California police. I know that his attorneys spent much of the O.J. Simpson Murder and Variety Show, Part I (the criminal trial) trying to portray the police as racial, evidence-planting incompetents.

But the truth is, the police saved O.J.'s life!

Flash back for a moment to the days immediately following the murder, when O.J. and his friend A.J. Foyt were eluding police questioning with their now-famous forty-five mile per hour ride on the expressway in A.J.'s Ford Bronco.

All of America witnessed this incredible debacle with footage taken by helicopters overhead, as O.J. and A.J. and L.M.N.O.P. proceeded with their stately ride, flanked from behind and front by squad cars.

There they were, driving on a major city expressway, **under the speed limit! …..in a passing lane! ….in LOS ANGELES!**

What most of America didn't see were the well-armed, frustrated Los Angeles commuters, impatiently milling around the police cars following O.J., just waiting til they could pass the squad cars on the shoulder of the highway, so they could get a good shot off at the imbecile going less than ten miles over the speed limit.

If the police really had a vendetta against O.J., all they had to do was let these rush hour drivers go.

Ha! Ha! Ha! Vigilante justice.

Driving School
Speaking of police, I was watching one of my favorite DVD's, *Jurassic Park*, which is a very good movie to watch when you're on your treadmill. Especially the chase scene with the T-Rex. That's when you'll be able to use the level ten setting that you figured there'd be no way you could ever use. Anyway, the paleontologist and two kids were watching the way a flock of ostrich-like dinosaurs ran from danger much as a school of fish does, zigging and zagging in perfect unison to escape predators.

What do police have to do with this, you ask? Well, I was reminded of this one morning as I sped along in a convoy of rush hour commuters ripping down an expressway in Chicago. We moved with drill-sergeant precision, weaving left and right to elude hazards like chuck-holes, Florida butterfly ballots, and slow drivers (defined as a driver on a Chicago expressway doing less than Mach Two during rush hour).

Suddenly, with unthinking synchronization, the whole school of commuters reacted as one to the presence of a predator. We slowed and merged to the right in perfect harmony, as the school moved to protect itself. The radar of the police is confused and cannot sort out a single violator.

Then the predator sees a straggler, and moves in with lights and speed and strength. The law of the jungle is upheld once again, as the predator brings down the hapless prey, which had been separated from the herd due to sickness or lack of coffee.

In this particular case, the lack of coffee was caused by poor service in a restaurant earlier in the morning. After the police let him go, the commuter, a man named Lynn Considerate Dryver, vowed to get that waiter back … after work … and after he went home to change out of his expensive, unique-treaded, Bruno Madagascar loafers.

Ethel

Ethel Nantz was my English teacher in high school. She was an older, distinguished woman, who kept a pretty firm handle on us scamps, yet she had our respect. Behind her back, she was affectionately called, 'Ethel,' but to her face, she was always, with no smirking, 'Mrs. Nantz.'

She taught college-prep English, and I remember some of her corrections very clearly. When she praised us, it was sparingly, and thus, an honor. I learned a lot from her, and although my English composition was probably better under her stern eye than now, I still feel she definitely helped me learn to express myself.

She is probably deceased now. If so, no one told me. I just figure she was not young when I knew her, and more than a quarter century has since gone by.

I wonder how many of the people that I used to know, sometimes well, are deceased now. I wonder if Mr. Robison (yeah, that's how they spelled it), my grade-school best friend's father, is alive. Or Mr. Snyder, who lived across the street from me when I was eight. My childhood friends Allan Sullivan, Bernie

Robison and Tim McQuiggle. It's impossible to keep up with everyone you ever knew or met, especially if you move around.

I saw a picture when a Tim McQuiggle was newly engaged. Was it the Tim that I grew up with? I studied the picture, looking for the child I knew way back when. I should have called, I know I should have. The odds of him moving to Chicago from Maryland were remote, but not impossible. But I didn't, and the reason is kind of sad. I have a full life right now, and even if it was my childhood friend, there is no room for reconnecting and keeping the contact new. This is sad, but this is life.

Once in a while you cross paths with someone you knew a long time ago, and you renew ties, sometimes simply at reunions. That's what reunions are for, to touch base, but only for that slice of memory. Nobody really expects to rekindle the spirit that burned in them decades earlier.

On this subject, they caught the Unabomber after years of eluding authorities. He is an ex-college professor who went off the deep end, sending bombs to universities and scholars for over twenty years. He's in his late fifties now, and the newspapers went back to his childhood for pictures and memories. How many peers of his have stories to tell, "I knew him! He was shy and smart, and used to go to fifth grade bomb-making class with me!"?

If he had done something useful with his talents, like bombing cigarette executives or telemarketers, he'd still be free today.

Animal Crackers
Who makes up jokes?

Especially those really sick, really funny jokes that happen after any event, whether good or bad. Jeffery Dahmer had barely digested before the pundits had created an armada of sick jokes, the only thing sicker being my inability to remember even one to

175

chronicle here. (Of course, I'm kidding; What do you find in Jeffery Dahmer's freezer? ..... Ben and Jerry!)

And once, when a plane was tragically downed in the Florida Everglades, I received a phone call **the same morning** from a friend, who wrapped up the conversation by asking, "What did the one Everglades alligator say to the other?"

With a sickening lurch in my stomach I respond desultorily, "I don't know, what?" And he gleefully blurts, "See, airline food isn't all that bad. Huhyuukk!!"

The only thing faster than the speed this gross joke was created, was the speed in which it traveled the U.S. Later that same morning, this joke was repeated to me by at least three people, none of whom knew the other. One was even out of state!

I'm kind of weird (not exactly a shocker, huh?) in that I cannot put a bad joke out of my mind until I repeat it to someone else. So I sauntered out into the office to repeat this joke to someone else, just so I can wipe it out (Ok, so I told my wife, too), and spied Tom.

"Tom," I said, "What did the one Everglades alligator..." He interrupted, saying "... See, airline food isn't all that bad. I heard the joke three times already," he explained. Then he says, "Here's one. Three women are walking down the street wearing potato sacks. How can you tell which is the hooker?" Happily I chirped, "The one whose sack says 'Idaho'! I heard that joke four times yesterday!"

Speaking of potatoes, everyone I know has some food, once a favorite, that he can't choke down anymore, because it was the last thing that went down before the stomach flu, food poisoning or a Michael Bolton concert. Mine is hotdogs.

About twelve years ago, I loaded up a hotdog with mustard and a ton of chopped onions, and in three bites glomped the whole thing. It was so good, I slorked another, then another. Little did I realize that my unnatural hunger was just my body loading up all the energy it could to sustain itself through the stomach flu it was busily incubating.

Well, you know what happened next. I ate those three hotdogs again, only in reverse. In fact, I think I upchucked **four** hotdogs! Twelve years later, and I still gag every time I get near a hotdog. I couldn't even watch Adam Sandler without provoking a gag reflex.

This drives me nuts (not the Sandler thing). Sandy had finally found a close relation to the food group that my kids actually like, that's easy to make, and I, the human food vacuum, can't stand it.

She can't get mad at me though. I tell her I'll eat a hot dog when I see her eating a piece of pumpkin pie (that's her flu food). Idea to bored scientists, next time a plane crashes in the Everglades, see if you can somehow make all the alligators catch the flu. Then they'll never want to have Purina People food again.

Chapter 16   Guys and misc. stuff that doesn't fit in any other category.

Songs

Imagine this, if you will.

Back in the caveman days, Grog, the first-ever percussionist, is banging on a couple rocks, busily banging out the very first rock song.

He's whacking away, hitting "A" notes, "G," "F-sharp." Shards of rock are flying, keeping a small, annoyed crowd at bay. A young cave youngster named Keith Richards is watching avidly.

Finally, his arms getting tired from the heavy rocks, Grog starts thinking to himself, "Hmmm, it's time to end this song."

But, he doesn't know how to do it. No human's ever created music before, and he isn't quite sure how it should end.

Should there be a grand finale, with a burst of rock crunching, followed by him kicking the rocks over and throwing them into the audience? That would help, maybe, and give him time to make a run for it.

But something about this doesn't stir his hairy Music Man soul. Likewise, Grog doesn't want to end it with just one sharp note, or even one flat note. He wants something else. Something different.

But what?

Then it hits him.

A stone. Ouch. Somebody threw a stone at him.

He ducks another, and then he figures out what to do.

He decides that he will end the song by repeating the final refrain over and over, over and over. And each time he repeats it, he will make it just a little quieter than the refrain before it, until it's gone.

So he starts, "Um, Urg, Ugh, Brah, er, Uh."

And he repeats it, "Um, Urg, Ugh, Brah, er, Uh."

Again, "Um, Urg, Ugh, Brah, er, Uh."

Another rock wings by his head, Grog ducks, persevering to the end, but even lower,

"Um, Urg, Ugh, Brah, er, Uh."

"Um, Urg, Ugh, Brah, er, Uh."

"Um, Urg, Ugh, Brah, er, Uh."

"Um, Urg, Ugh, Brah, er, Uh."

The music gets lower and lower, until finally it can't be heard.

As the music fades, Grog's lips are still moving. What the crowd hadn't realized is that Grog wasn't actually singing. His friend, Cronk, was hiding behind a nearby rock, and was doing the actual singing, since Grog's voice was known to sterilize newts at a hundred yards.

So as the music disappears, Grog has to keep moving his lips, until he's sure that not even the most sharp-eared caveperson can pick up the deception.

Bravely, he flaps his lips, alertly watching and listening.

When he judged the moment right, he stopped.

And bowed for the applause that was surely coming.

Fifteen minutes later, after the crowd had left, Cronk crept out of the rocks, and dragged his unconscious friend to safety. There he carefully stanched the bleeding, and wiped Grog's face until he recovered from the projectile hurled by Milli, or was it Vanilli?

Or Shania Twain?

Penny Earned

Are you as tired as I am of companies gypping themselves out of a penny? With all of the bankruptcies and store closings, it seems like businesses should do everything they can to try to survive. And what better place to start than by getting rid of the penny discount they give us, their beloved consumers, for all of their sales?

Think about it. Everything out there is for sale with prices like Big Macs for $1.99, televisions for $499.99, toasters for $29.99. I've even seen cars priced at $19,999.99.

Why do they do it? It's obvious, isn't it? They're just trying to help us, their customer. They realize that if we save a penny on **every** sale, then we are more likely than ever to respond with mad impulse buying. So, I guess, in a small way they are benefiting themselves. But that's just incidental, I'm sure. No way is it greed. And they surely aren't trying to fool us into thinking something is substantially cheaper than it really is, just by knocking a penny off it, right?

Ha! Ha! Ha! Ha!

No way they could think we're that stupid.

I just think it's wonderful that they are looking out for us this way. I mean, think about it, if I save just two million pennies I'll be able to pay cash for a car priced at $19,999.99. And I'll still have that extra penny left over, so that I can start saving for something else. Isn't this great? Think about the benefits to the economy.

But things are tough now, and I think it's important that we consider giving back for all their years of generosity. Think about how much money companies have lost over the years, gypping themselves out of a penny for each and every thing they sell. They must have sacrificed trillions of dollars by now.

I think we ought to start giving back! So, effective immediately, I'm calling for a national campaign where we all agree to spend that extra penny, to help save free-enterprise as we know it.

So let's tell them, consumers! Let's tell them that it's okay to call it a $20,000 car. We'll pay the extra penny! We'll do it, yes we will, because we care.

Zinckel

Speaking of the penny, I'm going to tell you something that you might not know about our little copper friend.

And that's just it... they aren't copper.

Whoa! Calm down, calm down. The world isn't upside down. Unless maybe you're in China, where we'd be talking about *juan, jiao* and *fens*. And we Americans would be the ones upside down. So, I guess, depending on your perspective, the world is upside down.

Anyway, the penny used to be made out of copper, but, since 1983, Lincoln head cents have been made with 97% zinc. The other three percent? Copper!!!

Yay!!

So there. Feel better? There actually is some copper in the penny.

So I'm sure now you're wanting confirmation that a nickel is made out of nickel. Don't worry, it is.

Whew.

In fact, 25% of a nickel is made out of nickel. And...

...wait! A quarter of the nickel is nickel? There's a quarter in a nickel? So what's in the other three quarters? Well, copper, of course. Huh? A nickel has more copper than a penny??!! This doesn't make cents, er, sense.

Hey. I'm just the messenger.

Can you take more? There's even more copper in the quarter than in the penny! The quarter used to be almost all silver, but since 1965, over 90% is copper, the rest nickel.

I know you're stunned. A quarter is made out of nickel and has more copper than a penny? Boy, this would mess up the exchange rate if it ever got out.

So how about the dime?

Well, it's partially made out of nickel (8%), and the rest is copper. Now you'd think that since there are two nickels in every dime, then a dime would be 50% nickel, and 50%, uh, another nickel; but it just doesn't work that way.

Okay, so let's review.

There are twenty-five pennies, which are no longer made out of copper, in every quarter, which is 90% copper. Two nickels go into every dime, but a dime is mostly made up of copper, which is what pennies used to be made of. A quarter is mostly copper, but doesn't go into a dime, which is also copper, but also partly nickel.

If you took all twenty-five pennies that go into a quarter, and melted them, you might have enough copper to make a quarter, but you couldn't make a quarter because you wouldn't have enough nickel.

A dime, two nickels and five pennies equals a quarter, and if you melt them down, you might get enough copper and nickel to make a quarter, unless it was an old quarter, which used to be made out of silver, in which case you'd have nothing.

Not only does a nickel go into a quarter, but there is a quarter nickel in every nickel. And though a nickel is 20% of a quarter, a quarter is only 8% nickel. There's some nickel in every nickel, and in every dime and quarter, but not in the penny. The penny was copper, but isn't anymore, and nowadays is made out of …. uh, zinc.

There is no such thing as a zinckel.

The Bad Luck Gods

Jerry, the maintenance guy at work, set up a very large ladder in the office so that he could climb up and give us a good view of his legs while his upper body was above the suspended ceilings. Fortunately, he wasn't wearing panties and garter. That I could see. Not that I was looking. But if he was, I would have had to look. Even though I didn't want to.

The ladder straddled the entire walkway in the middle of the office. In order to get past the ladder, you had to either squeeze by either side, or you could simply walk underneath, since there was clearance of a good seven feet.

It was in the path of my first cup of coffee, so I scooted by the opening on the right, telling myself it was safer to go around. Linda was behind me, and squeezed around, too. Meanwhile, Dennis simply detoured down another hallway. That's when Nancy came by. And, to our shock and amazement, she strolled **right underneath**, brazenly defying the Bad-Luck gods!

Isn't it amazing how intelligent people can, nevertheless, let superstitions get to them? Consider the athlete, who diligently performs the same rituals every day, under the guise of luck, hoping that their physical performance will benefit simply because of a ritual. And worse, be deathly afraid that they will become less capable if not.

Wade Boggs, one of the premier hitters of the 90's, religiously followed a superstitious ritual of eating a chicken on days that he played. Other athletes will wear the same socks for weeks if they are on a streak, without washing them. Mike Cueller, who won a Cy Young award in the 70's, refused to step on the top step of the dugout. And he insisted on picking the ball up from the mound when he came out each inning. One day, Boog Powell, who played first base, jogged by the mound, picked it up, and casually flipped it to Cueller, who dodged it like it was a mother-in-law. It landed at the feet of Brooks Robinson, coming up behind them. He helpfully picked it up and tossed it to Cueller, who again jumped back like a nervous mongoose. Finally, everybody got the hint, and let the shaken pitcher pick up the ball himself.

For us non-athletes, we have our own superstitions, or if not superstitions exactly, we still won't challenge certain of them. Like walking under ladders, stepping on cracks on the sidewalk, or breaking chain letters.

Who starts these chain letters? What kind of pleasure do they get out of beginning something that only preys on the dark fears of people? How can someone start one of these things? Do they receive visceral entertainment by imagining the terror or inconvenience they cause to the recipient? Like those techno-doofuses who think it's fun to create computer viruses.

Even I, who hopefully knows better, still feel a strong magnetic sensation on my fingers as I'm trying to let a chain letter slide from my fingers into the trashcan.

But still, I did it.

I'm safe.

And now I want it out of my office!

So, I took the trash can, and headed off to go dump it ......

....being very careful to avoid going under the ladder on the way.

Drugstores

They're putting up a drugstore near me.

Big deal, huh?

Well, it is. And you know why?

Because they're putting it right across the street from another drugstore.

Not only that, but within a four mile radius of my house, there are no less than five of just one kind of drug store, that I won't name (Walgreens). Now, an unnamed competitor (CVS) is setting up competing stores, sometimes right next to or across from their rivals.

What's going on here?

Our town is lacking in certain type retailers, like the ones I want, and have way too many of others, that I don't. For instance, banks have sprouted up like pimples on a teenager. Gas stations litter every corner. But it's the drugstores that are really doing most of the land grabbing.

Where we need a clothing store, we get a drugstore. Where we could use a hardware store, we get a drugstore. Where we could use a nice, new family dining establishment, we get a drugstore. Where we could use a drugstore, we get two drugstores.

So if you want money, no problem, you'll find a bank within hocking distance. You'll also have no problem finding a place to gas up. And, when you're ready to spend, no problem, there'll be a Walgreens nearby, ready to sell you toothpaste and cosmetics. Between banks, gas stations and pharmacies, we're running out of places to put McDonald's restaurants!

And worse, they're crossbreeding! I saw a gas station that had a twenty-four hour bank teller, and it also carries makeup and other stuff you get from pharmacies. And the pharmacies are carrying toys, groceries and wild game meat. And banks with, er, um. Anyway, I digress.

It's not that I have anything against Walgreens or other drugstores. We need them so that my daughters can spend my money on cosmetics. I'm just wondering if we need that many of them.

(Rumor has it that in some inner city neighborhoods, there's actually the possibility that soon drugstores will outnumber drug dealers!)

Nervy

Nerves are a wonderful thing if you can keep your kids off them. If you didn't have nerves, you couldn't move any muscles, and you wouldn't know if a mosquito was sucking out your life juices. Also, you could remove your finger while trying to cut a grapefruit during the Superbowl, and not realize you were bleeding to death the same way Buffalo used to bleed to death in the game. Actually, you might prefer bleeding to death as opposed to ever seeing the Bills in the Superbowl again.

It seems to me that God could have given us some kind of warning device other than pain. How about a loud noise or something? A gong sound, maybe.

Or that kind of feeling you get when you hit your funny bone, which stopped being funny about twenty years ago. Nowadays, I get this burning sensation when I hit my funny bone or when my foot falls asleep (while I am vapidly staring at a speaker in a seminar, who is imagining me in my underwear).

It used to just tingle when I set it off.   I actually liked the sensation, so I used to try to make my foot fall asleep, or whack my elbow on something. When it started becoming painful, I stopped.

Oh, I think I get it now.

Dreams

Everybody I know has had and remembers their own recurring dreams. I had two that came back time after time back when I was a kid. In the first one, I'm in a room full of beautiful, wonderful ..... chocolate Hershey's bars. Hey, I said I was a kid, remember?

No matter what kind of exotic candy my kids scarf down, Airheads, Scarfers, Screamers, Tongue-painters, etc., nothing beats the simplicity of a Hershey's bar. Take this from someone who wiped out half a coin collection just so I could stock up on candy one summer.

The other was my favorite, one of those flying dreams that I had as a kid, and never have any more. In this dream, I am walking near my grade school and a big gorilla type (not one of my lifesaving students, but very similar in gait and form) starts chasing me. I run away, and just as the gorilla is ready to grab me, and punish me for leaving the toilet seat up. I flap my arms and fly. But it's a hesitant fly, with me dropping back towards the Earth and ape-man, and shooting up just before he can grab at me again. Finally, gravity lessens its hold on me, hence I lose weight (though not mass), and I fly around the neighborhood, looking down at buildings, and pooping on pigeons.

Motion Sickness

When I was a boy, we'd go out in the woods, and climb saplings until they bent over from our weight. Still holding the poor thing, we'd jump up and down, floating high into the air, and coming back down slowly. We'd pretend we were astronauts on the (what I didn't know was doomed) Moon.

Then we'd go to the carnival and ride rides like the 'Lose Your Brat Slingshot' and the 'Stomach Vault,' not to mention the 'Show Us Your Dinner Launch' without even getting dizzy. Not anymore, though. Now I can't even get on the swing sets with my girls, without turning a deathly pale and hyperventilating. Meanwhile, they soar and dip and spiral while I grope my way back to the safety of my deck chair.

Dogs can do it too. We've all seen dogs riding in a Blazer or Yugo with its tongue (the dog's) flapping in the breeze. But have you ever seen a cat doing that? No way. They're like me. I read once that cats can't take the motion because their eyes are constantly trying to focus on the scenery as it whips by. They can't stand it, so they do the same thing I do when my family says they want to go to Great America, and ride its gut-wrenching torture chambers.

Hide, growl and hiss.

Stork Helpers

Grocery stores are getting into this polite thing now. I noticed that they are starting to carry full-service bank branches in the store. It's nice that they are finally acknowledging the high price of fish nowadays.

Seriously, though. I read that some grocery stores are establishing 'Stork' parking for pregnant women, near to the entrances.

This is great!

I can't think of a better idea. Even better, no guy can fake his way into using the space, huh?

Yep, I'd like to see that UCLA quarterback trying to pull that one off.

But how about those women, who are barely showing yet? Do they have to wait until they reach a certain girth? Or maybe they have some kind of breathalyzer that can determine the presence of morning sickness.

Of course, what we really need is stork delivery, where somebody will bring over pickles at two in the morning. Or a stork pretend-husband, who will take the wife's right cross in the hospital for having put her through HELL! Or stork middle-of-the-night feeders, who'll take care of things when Mom's got to sleep, and Baby Muffin just doesn't want to have anything to do with Dad.

And why can't the grocery store just go ahead and do some stork grocery delivery?

Save some time, huh?

...

How come it's always 'Happy' New Year, and 'Merry' Christmas? Why not Merry New Year? Or Happy Christmas? The same goes for Happy Birthday. Can't you have a Merry Birthday? Or how about Easters and Valentines? Can they be Merry, too?

And why not let them be exciting instead? I want people to wish me an Exciting Birthday! (mark your calendars for November 24).

Anyway, I made a resolution this year. I wouldn't wish happiness on anyone. Instead, I wished everybody an INTRIGUING New Year!

Chapter 17   On writing

Beanyweany
My sister-in-law, Cathy, who will remain nameless, wanted for awhile to write the next great romance novel, and penned the beginning parts. Hopefully, she will never read what I'm writing right now, because I read parts of her book, and, uh, well, let's say it's not her best work. She was trying way too hard to write, and wasn't succeeding in telling her story.

She made a mistake that Stephen King warned against in his book, *About Writing*. He gave an exercise where he asked the reader to imagine a room that has a cage in it. In the cage is a rabbit, with a green eight painted on its side.

Are you picturing this now? You are, aren't you?

If not, let's try again. There is a room that has a cage in it. In the cage is a rabbit, with a green eight painted on its side.

How about now? Anything taking shape in your brain? Still no?

Okay, there is a room that has a cage in it. In the cage is a rabbit, with a green eight painted on its side.

How about now?

Okay, that's better. Now think about your picture. Did I tell you what kind of cage? Is it metal or wood, glass or fence? What kind and color of rabbit? Does it have long ears, or those big floppy ones that fall over? It doesn't matter. I didn't have to give you the details. Your mind filled in all the blanks. You're no worse off for not seeing the picture the exact way another person does. But even better, you didn't get bogged down by reading a big long description of the room.

But back to my sister-in-law. It isn't that she isn't a good writer. She actually is, but more so when she lets the story just take off on its own. Several years ago, she penned a series of letters to my wife Sandy, before they found out how much fun it was to give money to Ameritech SBC, or whatever they call themselves this year; and in them she started including a first person story about a lady from a trailer park, and her daughter, Beanyweany.

This lady loved her trailer and loved everything about her white trash life (don't be offended, anyone. Please!) Anyway, she loved it when her man bent over and she could see his crack. A beer gut was just too damn sexy. They were on food stamps, and not at all bothered by it. They had schemes for buying cigarettes and beer on their little income. Then the social people took Beanyweany away from her, and she swore she would get her baby back. After all, the 'govmint' gave 'em good money for having a baby, and she couldn't afford to lose the extra benefits.

I won't ruin any more of the story in case she finally decides to publish it. It was one of the funniest things I'd ever read. I used to hang around the mailbox, just waiting for letters from Indianapolis. Then I'd hover over Sandy's shoulder, trying to catch up on Beanyweany's exploits, until she'd finally get exasperated, and just let me read first.

Wandering Eye
I always look at the wrong eye. I was in a service station paying for my gasoline, and the girl who was handling my payment was talking to me without looking at me. In fact, she was staring right over my left shoulder. Then I happened to glance at her other eye, and, to my surprise, it was boring right into mine! I started, and actually flinched backwards. I am predominantly left-eyed, and find I almost always look at

someone's right eye when I'm making eye contact, so usually I don't have any idea what the left eyes are doing.

I never got the nerve to ask, but I wonder if someone who has a straying eye actually gets two images, one from each eye. As you know, most of us combine the vision of both of our eyes, and we get a single vision. So, if you're somehow looking in two different directions, what kind of image are you receiving?

If I really strain, I can cross my eyes, and look at my nose, and for a short time, I see two images until I can merge the two together (you're trying this right now, right?). Maybe people who can look two different places at once, and still manage to drive a car (dart-free), are endowed with a brain superior to those of us who need two eyes just to see one image.

This reminds me of another story I would like to write sometime, if I can somehow master the energy. I want to write a story from a fly's point of view, with one of the premises being that flies are smarter than anyone suspects. First of all, consider what kind of sophisticated brain can transmit and interpret hundreds of different scenes they catch from their multiple-lensed eyes all at one time.

Most people think a fly has only four different overriding compulsions: 1) Flight away from threat; 2) Cruising for the cutest looking opposite sex; 3) Looking for something to land on to rest its wings; 4) Carrying out a search mission for the juiciest looking poop.

Actually, this is nowhere near the case. Consider, for a moment, the unique ability of flies to gain access to your house, no matter how small the opening. Leave a quarter-inch opening in your screen door, and you have seven flies buzzing around within twenty minutes. You might be inclined to think this is because flies are so numerous that they find the openings just stumbling into them simply by sheer volume of their population. So if this is true, why do you only find butterflies, bees, moths and wheelchairs in the grill of your car? There should be a plethora of flies crusting the whole front of your car every time you go out. Why aren't there? And how come when you're out on your bike, the only bugs hitting your face are beetles and mosquitoes? Besides the fact that they taste better.

I think it's because flies are actually intelligent. They see cars coming, consider the implications, then skip around us. I think the real reason they come into our house is their innate sense of curiosity. They are coming in to use the microwave over, watch TV, and read our books. They also have an insatiable taste for beer, so you tend to see more of them in the summer when you're out barbecuing and drinking brewskies.

Well, my book would explore the hidden intelligence of the normal housefly. It would show the tenderness as the new parent fly gazes into the multiple eyes of her beautiful, plump, adorable baby maggots, as she cleans their first tar-poop off their butt under the smug gaze of a nursefly.

You would get a first person view of just how to determine when poop is ripe, as the parent fly cruises the Crayola-decorated Baby Ruth's in my back yard. You would learn when poop is just the right consistency, ripe and fertile for maggot-growth. You would live a fly's life as you explore their deadly life and death struggles with frogs, dragonflies, and sucker-faced telemarketers.

Most people don't realize that flies sometimes win. Usually they try to tempt a frog into jumping after them right into the clutches of some of the large-mouth bass that flies sometimes hire as hit-fish.

Questions and Answers

I get a lot of writing practice by writing and editing the company newsletter where I work. And one of the best things about it is, in between all of the informational stuff, I tend to go off in a different, ah, direction.

The employees seem to like this, and have become quite creative in the Question of the Month segment. It started out pretty innocently, with questions relating to vacation policy, sales events, and whatnot (what's a whatnot?), but as you can see by the following segment, you're going to see that they really got into it, the whole point being to simply to try and stump me:

- Question: *If nothing sticks to Teflon, how does Teflon stick to the pan?*
- Answer: C'mon, give me a hard one!! You don't have to go far to get the answer to this seemingly impossible answer. The remarkable properties of Teflon are easily explained when you look at the scientific roots of this remarkable mineral. As you undoubtedly remember from high school physics class, Teflon is a natural element that is secreted from the adrenal glands of a salesperson. When applied to any hard surface, this mineral transfers to the surface the same qualities that salespeople use to give out work, even while work given to them is naturally repelled.

- Question: *When snow melts, where does the white go?*
- Answer: Only a monkey could answer this question, which has puzzled people for many years. Back n the old days, snow white simply went to sleep, to be stared at by dwarfs until kissed by a prince and awakened the following winter. Then one day, a Monkey, named Mike Nesmith, discovered a way to bottle it, and spread it on paper to cover mistakes.

- Question: *Why do customers prefer to come in ten minutes before closing?*
- Answer: Excellent question, and one that required considerable research. I conducted an in-depth scientific study (by sitting back in a chair and staring at the ceiling for forty-five seconds), and fathomed that all people want to be either the first at something, or the last at something. For instance, the baseball Mark McGuire hit for his 70th home run was auctioned for over one million dollars. However, if he hadn't hit numbers 1 through

69, number 70, by itself, wouldn't have been worth much at all. So each baseball he hit for a homerun during 1998 should be worth the same amount of money. But they aren't! Only the last one is! So I reasoned that people figure they get more value if they are the last one coming in the store to buy something. Proof of this can be seen the next morning when you see debris cluttering your parking lot. This is from people waiting in the parking lot for the last instant that they can conceivably squeeze into the store. As far as McGuire, though, since Bonds came around and broke his record, McGuire's home run balls aren't worth anything anymore.

- Question: *What direction should a ceiling fan rotate in summer and winter?*
- Answer: In a **circular** direction, in both summer and in winter. Sheesh, c'mon, give me a hard one.

- Question: *Why do kangaroos have their babies in their pouches … and how do they stay there when the mama is bouncing around?*
- Answer: I'll handle the second part of this question first, and with just one word … Velcro. As far as the first part, a kangaroo baby is called a joey, short for Joseph, who should have his own church. These marsupials are part of the macropod family (meaning big foot), which includes over 55 species, including certain NBA basketball players; and they keep their joeys in their pouches for two reasons: First, because a mother kangaroo is extremely organized. She is very creative at storing and packing items, like extra lipstick, napkins, and spare underwear. Because she is so economical, there is additional room for her joey. Also, it keeps them safe from their natural predators, the dingoes, since kangaroos really hate it when Elaine Benis (Seinfeld) says, "The dingo done got your baby."

- Question: *Why is lettuce crunchy?*
- Answer: I went to expert, Captain Crunch, for the answer to this sound-related question. The answer has its roots

in cellular biology, where we learn that the cellular structure of plants is rectangular, rather than oval, like the ones in animals, humans, water, and allegedly, salespeople. The physics of ripping these cells apart results in a wave-like physical reaction, that moves linearly through the air, and vibrates our eardrums. Our brains recognize these vibrations as noise. When lettuce begins to decay and wilt, the weakened cellular structure produces less vibration. However, some argue that if you rip lettuce in the woods, and no one is around to hear, it will make no noise.

- Question: *What's the difference between a reindeer and a deer?*
- Answer: As most people already know, a reindeer is actually a member of the deer family, *Cervidae*, subspecies *Rangifer Tarandus*, which means, "a deer in which Santa Claus controls by using reins." What fewer people know, though, is the female reindeer is the only female deer, other than Caribou, to have antlers, or horns. The purpose of these horns, of course, is so that reindeer pulling Santa's sleigh can honk at any airplanes that come too close.

- Question: *What's an armilary (we know what it is. Do you)?*

- Answer: Pa-shaw. Of course I do. I also know that the correct spelling is 'armillary'. This word dates back to the first King Larry (the Lion-Livered) of Armilia back in 1422. King Larry, as everyone knows, was the first to wear a prosthesis (fake) arm, after losing his right one in a tragic mishap involving a family of irate, but polite, gophers. Being a king, he was able to put together a large collection of wonderful arms to suit every occasion. Originally he kept the arms in the armory, but this confused his soldiers when they were looking for weapons and armor. So they made up a new name for the room where Larry's arms were stored called the Armillary (short for arm-of-Larry)

195

We'd spend a little more time on this, but we can tell by our sundial that it's getting close to lunch.

- Question: *Do the engineers at the downtown hotels use the same boxes the Christmas lights come in to put them away?*
- Answer: Yeah, right. And they believe in Santa, too.

- Question: *How and why do people get ulcers?*
- Answer: For this one, I went to Indianapolis, home of the Indy Five Hundred and Bobby Unser, ... what? Not 'Unser'? You're asking about 'ulcers?' Oh, um, sorry. I went to the sales manager, who, having caused many ulcers, is recognized as a leading authority on ulcers for this answer: Ulcers are caused by excess stomach digestive acids, which are triggered by physical or emotional stress, rather than by the arrival of food. Finding no food in the stomach to digest, these acids get bored and watch TV. Of course, this gives them the munchies, and since there's nothing to eat, they start eating the stomach linings themselves, which taste really good with Tobasco sauce. That's why your doctors tell you to stay away from Tobasco sauce and anything else that tastes good with stomach linings.

- Question: *Did the married man marry Miss Right as in always, or did he marry Miss Wrong as in never?*
- Answer: Um, I don't not get this not at all.

- Question: *Where did the phrase "Going to hell in a hand-basket come from?"*
- Answer: To answer this question, I pulled out our handy, dandy copy of Dante's *Inferno*, and while there was some good stuff in there, I couldn't find any mention at all about a basket. So I decided to look to the Classics for our answer. And of course, by classic, I mean classic children's stories. As you know, much truth and subliminal messages can be found in these stories, cleverly hidden behind symbolism and chaos. Like, for instance, the caterpillar in *Alice in Wonderland*. What the heck

was he smoking? But back to our question, there are two famous hand basket maidens in the classics, *Little Red Riding Hood* and Dorothy from *The Wizard of Oz*. Dorothy can be dismissed out of hand, because she simply used the basket to carry Toto and the Lone Ranger. So we turn our attention to Red Riding Hood. We know she was bad, of course, because she was a hood. And she wore red, **like the devil**. And she never took off the hood, so you couldn't see that **she had horns!** I'm glad this question was brought up, so we could expose this demoness for what she is. Warn your children, and never read this book again!

- Correction: It turns out the Question of the Month last month was phrased wrong. It should have said, "Did you marry Miss Right as in always right, or did you marry Miss Wrong as in never wrong? I apologize for my error. I'm guessing that the person who submitted this was either Miss Always Right, or Miss Never Wrong. And I'm never wrong, right?

- Question: *What gives a flower its scent?*
- Answer: Once again, we have to go to children's classic books for the answer to this question. I remember reading a story once about little fairy sprites that fly from flower to flower, with little atomizer bottles of Elizabeth Taylor perfume, and squirt subtle, tasteful spray onto the flowers' stamen, where the scent lingers, sending out aroma to attract male bumblebees. These bumblebees seek out the enticing odor and fly into the flower carpels, looking for cute chick bumblebees, inadvertently picking up globs of pollen as the bumble stumbles and trips over the flower's stigma. Finally, frustrated, they pick up the pollen, and realizing that their Queen will like it the way it smells, they fly it back to their hive, where they turn it into a sweet, sticky mess that they named Honey, in honor of their Queen.

- Question: *We want to know if anyone has a really great recipe for crabcakes.*

- Answer: Boy, did you come to the right place. Anyone who knows your friendly-neighborhood writer knows he was born in Maryland, home of the Chesapeake Bay blue crabs. Boy, this takes me back. Crabbing on the warm waters of the inland bay, dodging shallow sandbars, lemon sharks and horseshoe crabs. We'd throw the female crabs back in, because they were crabby. Sorry, just kidding. We'd do it to help keep the population up. Then we'd bring home three to five bushels of live crabs, steam them in huge pots, and invite a bunch of neighbors over for a crab-fest. We'd spread newspapers over the tables, and dump enormous piles of crabs on the table. You open them by the handy tab on their bottoms, pop the shells off, and spend hours picking through the white tender meat. Boy, those were the days! Oh, did I forget to answer the question? Oops, Sorry.

- Question: *Do dogs have taste buds? I ask that because I have two dogs, and they eat everything that hits the floor.*
- Answer: After exhaustive research, meaning I just dumped a bunch of stuff on the floor, I learned that my basset will eat tomatoes, zucchini, bread and crayons; but he wouldn't touch black olives, pickles or red gummy bears. This scientific study proved conclusively that he won't eat pickles. Also, as a handy tip, don't ever trust your dog to watch your food for you.

- Question: *Do drywall, oak trim and paint have any nutritional content?*
- Answer: Huh? Um, I guess. Termites seem to think so. I'm sure if you're building a gingerbread house or something. Never mind. I don't know. Go ask your dog.

- Question: *Are paint fumes actually harmful?*
- Answer: Darn tooting they are. If you get paint fuming mad, it's liable to roll itself up in balls, shove itself into a paint gun, then get itself shot at people.

- Question: *What do you call the floppy thing under a turkey's chin?*
- Answer: It's not a floppy, it's a CD-Rom. Just kidding. As any fan of the old Ally McBeal show knows, the loose skin under the chin is called a wattle. The turkey's wattle goes back to prehistoric days, back to when the turkey's ancestor, a shared relative of the pelican (pelicatussaur), ruled the piers and seaports of the dinosaurs. Recent archeological studies have proven that dinosaurs, contrary to thought, were actually quite accomplished sea persons, or sea monsters, as it were. As the ancient pelican gradually migrated further from the sea, and modified its diet by no longer eating fish, its wattle gradually decreased until it shrunk to the vestigial skin flap we see on the modern turkey.

(Yeah, I'm a blast to work around, doncha think?)

Chapter 18   The origin of Guy

You'd figure that this would be in the front of the book, but I'm a guy, so I decided to be perverse about it. But you can't read about guys without knowing just where the word came from.

Guys

If you're like me (hopefully not, for your sake), sooner or later you start wondering about things that most people take for granted. Like the word 'guy,' for example.

I use the word a lot, especially to describe myself.

Yep, I'm a guy.

Maybe you're a guy, too. If you are, though, you're probably not going to like what's coming up. If you aren't, try not to snicker. It's not polite.

And if you're from England, you aren't going to hear anything you don't already know. But for the rest of us...

Once upon a time, there was a guy named Guy Fawkes.

True story, by the way.

Guy Fawkes was born in 1570 in England, when Queen Elizabeth ruled the proud island. A Protestant, she pretty much roughed up those of the Catholic faith, and when she died in 1603 Catholics were hoping they'd receive better treatment under King James I.

Well, that didn't happen.

So a guy named Robert Catesby...

Wait, before we go on, you need to know something. In 1603 guys were not yet called guys. The phrase didn't exist yet. There were no such thing as guys. Don't misunderstand me. There were guys. They just weren't called guys yet.

Anyway, back to the story.

A guy named Robert Catesby, before guys were called guys, came up with a bright idea. He got together with a bunch of frat buddies, including a guy named Guy Fawkes, swilled a bunch of brews (tea, probably, since, after all, we are talking about England), and came up with a bright idea. Waving around a turkey leg, he said, "Hey guys (even though they weren't called guys yet), let's blow up Parliament!"

You can tell that he's a guy, right?

So were the other guys, because they all thought it was a great idea.

They got a bunch of dynamite, and planted it in a cellar under the House of Lords, and got ready to set off the fireworks. Guys like fireworks.

But, one guy, after thinking it over, sent an anonymous letter to one of his buddies, Lord Monteagle, who happened to be a member of the government, warning him to stay away from Parliament on November 5th.

Well, of course after that word leaked, and the King's forces stormed the cellar the night before and found one Guy Fawkes in the cellar singing the rowdy drinking song, "Ninety-Nine Bottles of Beer on the Wall," surrounded by thirty-six barrels of gunpowder (on the Wall).

Well, the authorities didn't see the humor in the whole thing, so they tortured Guy by making him watch re-runs of Three's Company. Then, mercifully, they put him to death before he started acting like Suzanne Somers.

But all the guys of England were feeling a little gypped, since they didn't get their fireworks display. So the next day, they started a huge bonfire.

On the first anniversary, they did it again.

Then again. Soon, people started throwing effigies onto the bonfires. Effigies of Guy Fawkes, the Pope, Britney Spears.

They did it every year, and the tradition got bigger and bigger, with fireworks, brats and square dancing. And preparations included making a dummy of Guy Fawkes, that they called "the Guy." Children would carry their 'Guy' around, and beg for 'a penny for the Guy,' using the money to buy fireworks for the night's fun.

I'm not kidding.

So what's it say for guys that we're named for a dummy?

And what's it say for guys, that even if we knew it, we'd wear it like a badge of honor?

The final word, period
A small number of people have gotten a peak at this book, and the universal response was "huh?!" Though usually the next thing they'd say after 'huh?!" is "Dude, you need help."

But a few looked beyond the obvious, and wondered where I got all the weird ideas. It's not really hard, and it's actually something you can practice.

Look around. That's all it takes.

Don't accept what people tell you.

It's okay to stretch your mind, like wondering about why trees don't break from the weight of leaves. Heck, I wonder this every time I rake.

And when you think back to science classes, you realize that they don't teach you things you really need to know. Like how there are trillions and trillions of molecules between your eyes and the pages of this book, yet you can clearly see these words right through them. Pretty freaky, huh?

Then, of course, I'd start wondering what the heck an 'illion' was.

And when I thought more about the molecules, I'd try to apply some of what I know to the whole thing. For instance, a few years ago there was an explosion that rattled my entire house. I frantically ran downstairs to see if it was my furnace or hot water heater, since the sound seemed to have come from my basement.

It wasn't until later that I'd learned that the explosion had taken place on a barge going down the river in Joliet, fifteen miles away.

Of course, this got me to thinking about how a sound wave can create a physical presence, shattering windows miles away from the incident. Did one molecule shove another, then another, then another, radiating from all directions from the explosion? And did they say 'excuse me' for shoving each other? And then, like some madcap Rave, would the second one shove the first one back, creating what's known as an aftershock?

That's how it happens. And that's how this book happened.

I never realized how hard it is to name a book. I always figured the right name would just sock you in the head. The problem with my book is that there is no real subject, other than how a guy perceives the world around him. I mention crabs a few times, so thought of calling this, "Sex-Crazed Crabs and Random Thoughts." And because I discussed birds quite a bit, I considered "Twenty-Two Robins and a Flock of Seagulls." Sandy didn't like this one, nor "And the Spittle Flew."

Likewise, two others were shot down at work, "How to Destroy the Moon," (they thought people would think this was an instructional manual), and my personal favorite, "The Best Zebra-Watching Vantage Point." My other favorites, "The Clammy Wet Handshake and Other Defenses," "The Accidental Book," and "Bathroom Whiz-dom, a book you should read sitting down," were summarily dissed.

I also liked, "Because God Likes Green," "Huh??!!", "Tangents and Other Stray Thoughts" and "The Story of Floyd."

I came up with something much simpler. Simple, stupid stuff. Something we can all relate to, some more than others.

Of course I didn't stick with this, either.

And you're lucky, you can read the book and move on. But these thoughts, and others, are trapped in my head, bouncing crazily back and forth between my cerebral cortex and parietal lobe like a mutant Superball.

And, worse, because the Superball's in my head, I can't even play with it.

...

So let's wrap this up by talking about endings a little bit.

What?

You know, endings.

For example, you know you're at the end of this book, because there are more pages in your left hand than in your right hand, unless, of course, you're looking at a copy that's been translated into Arabic.

So where does it make more sense to discuss this?

What do you like more, beginnings or endings?

Do you like the beginning of a romance, when everything is scintillating and your nerves twang whenever she/or he is anywhere near you? Or would you hate the beginning, especially blind dates, where you learn that your date's breath could stun a moose?

There are beginnings of everything and nothing. The first bite of a hotdog, compared to the last bite of a hotdog. Does beer taste better with the first sip, or after you're stoned as a Blarney rock?

Would you rather be starting school, or finishing it?

If you really think about it, sometimes you prefer the end of something, and sometimes you prefer the beginning of something. And if you eat Oreos, you like that stuff in between.

Sometimes it makes no difference at all. Sometimes the beginning of a book is the best part, sometimes the ending is. Whether you like one or another is totally personal preference. Then again, some people only eat the middle of their corn on the cob.

Where am I going with all of this?

Oh, yeah. Some things have no endings. Like a circle. Or the universe. Or the hot air from a politician. The universe goes on and on forever, with no ending. If there is an ending, there has to be something after, so there really is no ending, right?

A circle, rather than ending, is more like an endless loop, like when you're driving around a mall looking for a way out.
Not so for this book, though.
There is an ending. A place where you can say, "Ah, I'm done," close it, and go off to do something productive.
So, without further ado, may I present ….
The end.

On February 5, 1998, the Psychic Friend's Hotline went bankrupt. Don't you think they should have seen this coming?

Norm's books
Bonk & Hedz (a caveman ... and woman...story)
The Adventures of Guy
The Next Adventures of Guy
Fang Face
WereWoof
The Guy'd Book, why we leave the seat up... and other stuff

www.normcowie.com

Some of Norm's reviews:

on Fang Face and its sequel WereWoof

"I loved this book, fangs and all." ~ Best selling author James Rollins
"... fantastically funny." ~ BookLoons
"This book sucks ... in a most delightful way. Don't miss this gem.." ~ Shane Gericke, national bestselling author
"... an amusing teen vampire tale..." ~ Five-starred review ~ Harriet Klausner, Amazon's #1 book reviewer
"...genuinely funny..." ~ Taliesin - The Vampire's Lair

on The Adventures of Guy and its sequel The Next Adventures of Guy

"... humorous fantasy at its best..." ~ Armchair Interviews (Amazon Top reviewer)
"...LOL funny" ~ Beverly at Publisher's Weekly
"No topic is safe from Cowie's incredible wit and entertaining turn-of-phrase." ~ Pop Syndicate (named one of Pop Syndicate's Top Ten Books of 2007)
"...hilarious mishaps...." ~ Joliet Herald News
"Hilarious, witty and oozing with snappy sarcasm..." ~3Rs Bits, Bites & Books
"Don't bother picking up this one if you've no sense of humor" ~ Amanda Richards, Amazon Top Reviewer
"Everything in the book is so true, you can't help but laugh in agreement." ~ Roundtable Reviews
The Next Adventures of Guy, winner "Best Sci-Fi Fantasy" in Preditors and Editors readers choice award

15497584R00120

Made in the USA
Charleston, SC
06 November 2012